# POETRY IN THREE DIMENSIONS

Reading, Writing, and Critical Thinking through Poetry

## BOOK TWO

by Carol Clark and Alison Draper

Educators Publishing Service
Cambridge and Toronto

- To our colleagues at Crystal Springs Uplands School, Hillsborough, California, and those at neighboring Bay Area schools for their constructive comments and encouragement of our work in progress.
- To the students in the sixth and eighth grades at the Crystal Springs Uplands School, the students in the fifth and sixth grades at the Crystal Springs Uplands School Summer Enrichment Program, and the students in the sixth grade at Columbia Middle School, Berkeley Heights, New Jersey, for their thoughtful response to the poems in this collection and for their enthusiasm.
- To the student photographers, Erika Carrillo, Lindsay Greene, Abe Nachbaur, and Lindsay Zwicker, who have generously allowed us to use their photographs in this book and to their teacher at Crystal Springs Uplands School, Audrey Shehyn.
- To Norma Fifer, our friend and mentor, for her guidance, support, and love of language, which continue to inspire us.
- To our families for their helpful criticism, patience, sense of humor, and interest in our pursuit.



Book design by Persis Barron Levy

Printed in the U.S.A.
ISBN 0-8388-2368-8

# CONTENTS

SET 2. CHANGE



## THE THIRD DIMENSION: RELATIONSHIPS

SET 1. FAMILY



SET 2. TRIBUTE



## CLOSE-UPS OF TWO POETS: POEMS AND QUESTIONS

### EMILY DICKINSON AND YUSEF KOMUNYAKAA

SET 1. THE POEMS OF EMILY DICKINSON (1830–1886)



SET 2. THE POEMS OF YUSEF KOMUNYAKAA (1947– )

# • INTRODUCTION FOR STUDENTS •

Imagine life as a frog in an aquarium. Learn about the struggles and perseverance of an immigrant field worker, inspired by her dreams of the future. View the world from a new point of view—that of a skydiver observing earth. Experience the pain of war and racial prejudice, and how it feels to fight for freedom. Celebrate the accomplishments of athletes, musicians, and families. In Book 2 of *Poetry in Three Dimensions* we invite you to explore all of these subjects—and more, and to enjoy the form and rhythm that poetry offers.

## WHAT YOU WILL FIND IN THIS BOOK

You will see that the poems in this book are divided into five main sections. There are three topics or *Dimensions:* Creatures, Journeys, and Relationships. Within each of these *Dimensions,* the poems are further divided into subtopics called *Sets.* In addition, we have included two sections called *Close-Ups* and *Classic Models.* In *Close-Ups* we offer four poems by Emily Dickinson and four poems by Yusef Komunyakaa. All of the poems in *Dimensions* and *Close-Ups* are by American poets writing in the nineteenth or twentieth centuries. In *Classic Models,* you will find examples of traditional "fixed form" poems that poets have written throughout the ages in Europe, Asia, and the United States. Book 2 of *Poetry in Three Dimensions* also includes several modern variations on these traditional forms.

## WHAT YOU WILL DO

After each poem in the *Dimensions, Close-ups,* and *Classic Models* sections, you will find two questions encouraging you to investigate the structure or language of the poem and the literary devices used by the poet. We also ask you to consider what the poem means and how this meaning relates to your personal experience. For many of the poems, we have provided activities designed to stimulate your creativity by asking you to write a poem or draw a picture, engage in some form of research, or compare and contrast different works.

*Poetry in Three Dimensions, Book 2,* is a collection of works by Americans: African Americans, Asian Americans, European Americans, Hispanic Americans, and Native Americans. Our society has been enriched by the contributions of all of these groups. Through *Poetry in Three Dimensions, Book 2,* we hope you will celebrate our shared heritage and enjoy thinking about the many ways human beings are different and the same.

## THE FIRST STEP—GETTING THE FEELING OF A POEM

The first characteristic of poetry that most students notice is its brevity. Poems are short! Like small treasures, they are also packed with gem-like words and phrases that appeal to your senses. When you read a poem, you will hear and see, and possibly taste, touch, or smell the images that the poet puts before you. Sometimes, reading and listening to poetry is similar to listening to music. Even when you hear a song in a foreign language, you can feel the expression that the composer is conveying to you.

Poems, even complex poems, can have a similar effect on the reader. Don't give up if a poem doesn't "make sense" to you after an initial reading. First, try to express what the poem makes you feel in the same way you would for a song you've heard for the first time. Write your feelings in your poetry book, right next to the poem's title. Then use the reading, writing, and thinking tools suggested below to help you find ways to understand why and how the poem makes you feel a certain way.

## IDENTIFYING THE SPEAKER IN A POEM

When poets write poems, sometimes they imagine what it must be like to observe the world from the point of view of a creature or a person who has had experiences very different from their own. This creature or person is the observer looking at the world conveyed to you through the poet's words. In this book, we refer to this observer as the **speaker**, and sometimes we refer to the **point of view** of the speaker. In other words, the speaker and the poet are often not the same.

To understand a poem, you must know who or what is telling you the story, expressing a feeling, or describing a scene in a poem. Is the speaker a boy or girl, a man or woman, a dog, an objective observer (such as a newspaper reporter), someone looking back on the past, or someone looking ahead to the future? Even if a poet uses an "I" as a speaker, that speaker may have a very different point of view from that of the poet.

The poet is like an invisible puppeteer or someone who manipulates the strings of a marionette and makes the puppet or marionette speak and move. The poet creates the words that the speaker speaks. He or she is the master artist behind the words. When we refer to the feelings or ideas that a poem creates, we refer to the speaker's feelings or ideas, not those of the poet.

## UNDERSTANDING POETIC DEVICES

Like all artists, poets use **techniques** to make their art appealing and understandable to the reader. We call these tools **poetic devices**. In the "Glossary of Poetic Terms," you will find helpful explanations for all the poetic devices and techniques to which we refer in the questions.

The questions on a poem might ask you to identify and explain the effects of these devices. For example, if a question asks you to find **figures of speech** such as **similes** in a poem, you will need to look for phrases that employ the words *like* or *as*, such as "My heart is like a rose." After you find the similes and circle them in the poem, you are ready to ask, "What do they make me see or feel?"

The questions might also ask you to put brackets around the main sections of the poem. The sections of the poem, sometimes determined by stanzas, sometimes by punctuation, and sometimes only by a slight change in the types of words or images in the poem, constitute its **structure**. Like a well-planned house, a poem is built on a solid foundation, and it may have a simple or an intricate architecture. Locating the parts of the poem's structure is similar to looking at a blueprint for a building. The parts enable you to see how the poet has organized the main ideas of the poem.

## THE FIVE SENSES—GETTING THE PICTURE

The language of poetry often appeals to the five senses: sight, sound, touch, smell, and taste. While the last two may appear rarely in a poem, the first three are very common. Frequently, an Activity assignment will ask you to draw a picture of a poem. After you read a poem, try to make a picture in your head, or a series of pictures, that reflect the words of the poem. These pictures are the **imagery** of poetry. Sometimes the imagery involves the process of comparison in **figures of speech** such as **metaphor**, **simile,** or **personification**. These comparisons in figures of speech help you to make sense of the pictures in your head by comparing one thing to another.

If the words use **rhyme** or **rhythm** or repeated consonant or vowel sounds to create a feeling in a poem, you are hearing as well as seeing the picture in your head. Such a poem is a like a movie with sound. If the other senses are involved, you may be stepping into the "virtual reality" of a poem. For example, if you can hear as well as picture "the arc of a flat stone skipping/in the hollow trough of a wave" in Garrett Hongo's "What For," you have entered the scene of the poem and have let your senses stimulate your imagination.

When you first read a poem, circle or underline words that appeal to your senses. Write those senses down in the margin of the poem, and they will serve as reminders of how the poem works.

## THE READER

Once you have an idea of the picture or the feelings expressed in a poem, you are on your way to interpreting the poem's meaning. Sometimes a question asks you to explain how a specific poetic device works. For example, you might be asked about the **simile** in "My love is like a red, red rose," and you would probably answer that the image uses a direct comparison between the speaker's feeling of love and a beautiful red flower. You might also be asked what a word or title *implies*, or why there is a *contrast* between two images. To respond to such questions, you must figure out how the poem works—how the poetic devices contribute to your understanding of the feelings and ideas expressed in the poem.

A second question might ask you for your *interpretation, personal response,* or *opinion.* You are ready for these questions after you have tried to figure out how each piece of the poem fits into the big picture.

A question on *interpretation, personal response,* or *opinion* asks you, the reader, to take a stand on the poem. What do you think or feel about a particular subject and why?

## USING THE BOOK

*Poetry in Three Dimensions, Book 2,* is easy to use.

- Beside the questions that follow each poem, you will find space for writing answers to the questions.
- The footnotes that accompany the poem will help you to understand difficult words and **allusions**.
- Before you do your first assignment in the book, examine the Contents to see where you can go to help yourself.
- The Glossary of Poetic Terms will help you to understand questions that ask you to identify examples of specific devices or techniques in a poem. (These devices or techniques are always indicated in **bold** type.)
- The Activities section, which follows the poetry sections, contains additional assignments that your teacher may ask you to complete.
- The section titled About the Poets gives you biographical information about the authors that you may find useful in helping you to understand the context of a particular poem.
- The Index will help you locate authors and titles.

We hope you will find both challenge and pleasure in reading the poems in this book.

**Carol Clark and Alison Draper**

## The Secret

Denise Levertov (1923–1997)

Two girls discover
the secret of life
in a sudden line of
poetry.

I who don't know the
secret wrote
the line. They
told me

(through a third person)
they had found it
but not what it was
not even

what line it was. No doubt
by now, more than a week
later, they have forgotten
the secret,

the line, the name of
the poem. I love them
for finding what
I can't find,

and for loving me
for the line I wrote,
and for forgetting it
so that

a thousand times, till death
finds them, they may
discover it again, in other
lines

in other
happenings. And for
wanting to know it,
for

assuming there is
such a secret, yes,
for that
most of all.

1964

# THE FIRST DIMENSION: CREATURES

PHOTO BY ERIKA CARRILLO

## Proof

Julia Alvarez (1950– )

Papi brought home a puppy
stained with ink spots, a gift
from a grateful American
whose tonsils he'd taken out.
Alone with the speckled puppy
I tried rubbing off the spots
until Looky yelped in pain.
The maids wouldn't come close
fearing the devil's work.
Only Gladys like doubting Thomas[1]
touched the dots wanting proof
the dog wasn't just another
made-in-the-USA[2] gadget.
I, too, doubted he was real.
Until in a book Tía brought
from a trip to Nueva York,[3]
I saw towers touching the sky,
a giant virgin with tiny people
walking inside her halo.[4]
I showed the pictures to Gladys
who wet her finger to turn
the pages as I had taught her.
Her hand flew up to her forehead
tracing a sign of the cross.[5]
*Let's make each other a promise—*
I nodded, eager for pacts,
especially those confirmed
with blood or dare-you swigs
from coca-colas kept for company.
*Swear that whoever goes first*
*to the USA land of marvels*
*will come back and report*
*if all of these are just stories.*
Outside from his new pen
Looky barked as living proof
the extraordinary was alive
right under our very noses.

1995

1 doubting Thomas — a reference to the disciple of Jesus in the New Testament of the Bible. Thomas was known for his skepticism about Jesus's miracles.

2 made-in-the-USA — on a garment or product, a printed label identifying the United States as the country of origin on items imported to Mexico and other places outside the United States.

3 Nueva York — Spanish for New York City.

4 virgin . . . halo — a reference to familiar images of the Virgin Mary (the mother of Jesus in the Christian religion) in paintings and sculpture. It is also a reference to the Statue of Liberty.

5 sign of the cross — a reference to a solemn religious gesture made by some Christians as a symbol of Jesus's resurrection.

## Questions for **Proof**

1. Identify the **point of view** of the **speaker** (her age and cultural identity). What view of America does she suggest in such **images** as "made-in-the-USA gadget" (line 13), "towers touching the sky" (line 17), and "the USA land of marvels" (line 32)?

2. At the end of the poem, what does the **speaker** discover about the "puppy / stained with ink spots" (lines 1–2), and what has helped her make her discovery? Explain the poem's title.

**SEE ACTIVITIES, PAGE 104.**

## Deer in the Bush

Chana Bloch (1940– )

They come down
in the mornings, sniff
the green edges of our lives,
munch the hydrangeas.

Shadows let them.
They step
in a pool of shade,
their legs spindly as twigs,

inquisitively
nosing our flowers,
nudging us out on the porch
to watch them

watch us for a sign.
They do not blink.
They measure our moving towards them
and won't be fooled,

letting their pleasure wilt on the bush
till they can be sure of us.
Nothing between us now, but
wood and air.  Wait,

I can see a buck
up on his hind legs,
wrestling a branch down, his velvet mouth
dripping berries.

He's at home in our patch of seasons
like an old uncle
who comes when he pleases, and keeps
the secrets of the tribe.

1985

## Questions for **Deer in the Bush**

1. Explain "sniff / the green edges of our lives"(lines 2–3): who is sniffing and what are the "green edges of our lives"? What examples of "green edges" can you think of in your own life or in someone else's?

2. Why does the **speaker** demand our attention at the end of the fifth **stanza** with the command "Wait," (line 20)? What has changed in her perception of the relationship between the deer and the people who watch them?

**SEE ACTIVITIES, PAGE 104.**

## White Panther

### Gene Frumkin (1928– )

I camped last night in the ravine
northeast of Taos[1] where the white panther
was rumored several times in recent months.
During the night I was counseled twice,
once by footfalls outside the tent
and later by an Indian, tall and hatchet-nosed,
eyes brown and calm as a bear's.
He said, "Get up and look outside."

I opened the flap and there was the moon,
stony cold, slanting through my dream.
The spruce and pine were still.
The fire I'd built to cook my late meal
was a grey cloud of ashes.
I remembered the footfalls and thought,
"Of course, it was the white panther!
God has consented to believe in me."

When I awoke in the morning
a crow had gotten wedged into my chest.
His wings smashed about furiously
and his "caw-caw" was the voice
of the Indian laughing at me.
Despite his counsel I had slept through
my welcome. There is no white panther
northeast of Taos, not any more.

1976

---

1 Taos — a town in northern New Mexico surrounded by mountains and desert.

## Questions for **White Panther**

1. In the margin to the right of the poem, label each **stanza** according to its main idea. What stage in the **speaker's** thoughts about the white panther does each stanza represent?

2. Why does the **speaker** use the phrase "not any more" (line 24) to emphasize that "There is no white panther / northeast of Taos" (lines 23–24)? How does the speaker's experience during the night with "footfalls" (line 5) and "an Indian" (line 6) lead him to an understanding about reality and imagination, as revealed in stanza 3?

**SEE ACTIVITIES, PAGE 104.**

## Lost

Naomi Shihab Nye (1952– )

notices flutter
from telephone poles
until they fade

OUR SWEET TABBY AFRAID OF EVERYTHING

BIG GRAY CAT HE IS OUR ONLY CHILD

SIBERIAN HUSKY NEEDS HIS MEDICINE

FEMALE SCHNAUZER WE ARE SICK WITH WORRY

all night I imagine their feet
tapping up the sidewalk
under the blooming crepe myrtle
and the swoon of jasmine
into the secret hedges
into the cool dark caves
of the banana-palm grove
and we cannot catch them
or know what they are thinking
when they go so far from home

OUR BELOVED TURTLE RED DOT ON FOREHEAD
VEGETARIAN NAME OF KALI

please please please

if you see them

call me call me call me

1998

## Questions for **Lost**

1. Underline phrases that reveal the **speaker's** feelings about the lost creatures in the notices.

2. Why does the poet capitalize all the letters of some words and none of the letters of other words?

**SEE ACTIVITIES, PAGE 104.**

## Glass Specialty

A. R. Ammons (1926–2001)

The redbird, nesting
in the nearby
yewbush, has found

A fluttering rival in
the garage window: pecking
as at a nectar of hatred,

He (not a hummingbird)
thrashingly sustains
himself before his image:

weakened to the ground, he
comes back up, the ruffling
rival there every time.

1992

## Questions for **Glass Specialty**

1. What does the redbird actually see in the "garage window" (line 5), and why are the references to a "fluttering rival" (line 4) and "ruffling / rival" (lines 11–12) humorous to the **speaker** who is observing the bird?

2. In this short, sentence-long poem, which words, **images**, and **figures of speech** help you understand the ancient Greek myth of Narcissus that the poem presents from a new perspective? (In this myth, a young man named Narcissus falls in love with his own reflection in a fountain. Thinking that the reflection is a female nymph, he jumps into the water to reach her and drowns, eventually turning into the white flower called "narcissus.")

**SEE ACTIVITIES, PAGE 104.**

## Credo[1]

### Maxine Kumin (1925– )

I believe in magic. I believe in the rights
of animals to leap out of our skins
as recorded in the Kiowa legend;[2]
directly there was a bear where the boy had been

as I believe in the resurrected wake-robin,[3]
first wet knob of trillium to knock
in April at the underside of earth's door
in central New Hampshire[4] where bears are

though still denned up at that early greening.
I believe in living on grateful terms
with the earth, with the black crumbles
of ancient manure that sift through my fingers

when I topdress[5] the garden for winter. I believe
in the wet strings of earthworms aroused out of season
and in the bear, asleep now in the rock cave
where my outermost pasture abuts the forest.

I cede him a swale of chokecherries[6] in August.
I give the sow and her cub as much yardage
as they desire when our paths intersect
as does my horse shifting under me

respectful but not cowed by our encounter.
I believe in the gift of the horse, which is magic,
their deep fear-snorts in play when the wind comes up,
the ballet of nip and jostle, plunge and crow hop.[7]

I trust them to run from me, necks arched in a full
swan's S, tails cocked up over their backs
like plumes on a Cavalier's[8] hat. I trust them
to gallop back, skid to a stop, their nostrils

level with my mouth, asking for my human breath
that they may test its intent, taste the smell of it.
I believe in myself as their sanctuary
and the earth with its summer plumes of carrots,

its clamber of peas, beans, masses of tendrils
as mine. I believe in the acrobatics of boy
into bear, the grace of animals
in my keeping, the thrust to go on.

1992

1 credo — a formula of belief.

2 Kiowa legend — a legend of the Kiowa tribe of Plains Indians formerly of Colorado, Oklahoma, Kansas, New Mexico, and Texas. (The legend is summarized in line 4 of the poem.)

3 wake-robin — a common name for the trillium plant (also known as jack-in-the-pulpit), which grows wild in mountain meadows and forests.

4 topdress — to cover a garden with branches, bark, or other loose organic material to protect plants from harsh winter weather

5 New Hampshire — a state in the northeastern part of the United States, known for its forests, mountains, and wildlife.

6 chokecherries — bitter fruit from a flowering North American shrub or tree.

7 crow hop — a reference to the light, dance-like movements of a crow.

8 Cavalier's hat — a hat with a feather, such as those worn by the Cavaliers who were supporters of King Charles I during his struggles with the English Parliament in the seventeenth century.

## Questions for **Credo**

1. In the space to the right of the poem, make a list of the beliefs (credos) stated by the **speaker** in the poem. Then, in the space below, reorganize the items on your list according to their similarities. What do the categories of belief have in common?

2. The poem begins with a reference to a Kiowa legend about a bear leaping out of the skin of a boy, "I believe in the rights / of animals to leap out of our skins" (lines 1–2). The poem ends with a reference to the same legend, "I believe in the acrobatics of boy / into bear" (lines 34–35). What changes for the **speaker** have occurred between the two references? Why is the legend important to her experience?

**SEE ACTIVITIES, PAGE 104.**

## Moles

Mary Oliver (1935–   )

Under the leaves, under
the first loose
levels of earth
they're there—quick
as beetles, blind
as bats, shy
as hares but seen
less than these—
traveling
among the pale girders
of appleroot,
rockshelf, nests
of insects and black
pastures of bulbs
peppery and packed full
of the sweetest food:
spring flowers.
Field after field
you can see the traceries
of their long
lonely walks, then
the rains blur
even this frail
hint of them—
so excitable,
so plush,
so willing to continue
generation after generation
accomplishing nothing
but their brief physical lives
as they live and die,
pushing and shoving
with their stubborn muzzles against
the whole earth,
finding it
delicious.

1978

## Questions for **Moles**

1. According to the **speaker** in lines 1–17, in what sort of environment do moles thrive? Which **images** especially provide a vivid picture of the moles' habitat?

2. Note that the poem is composed of just two sentences. Which **images** in the poem particularly make you think about "accomplishing nothing" (line 29) and the fact that the moles go on for generations? Why is this contrast **ironic**?

## Aquarium

Nancy Willard (1936– )

The frog who works out
in the clean gym of the water

has neglected his arms.
Flexed,[1] they are skinny as worms.

It's his legs he cares for;
plié[2] perpetual,

muscles in baggy pants.
What charm when he extends

the ribbed fans of his feet,
as if a spider sat on a breath,

testing the weight of it.
Who in the corps of carp

or the schools of fantails
and angelfish, jewels

of the first water,
can match his leaps?

1972

---

1 flexed — referring to the dance term *flex*, which means to hold the foot at a 45-degree angle (perpendicular) to the leg.

2 plié — a dance position in ballet in which the dancer, standing erect, turns out the legs at the hip and bends the knees, making a V shape with the thighs. The word is derived from the French verb *plier*, meaning *to bend*.

## Questions for **Aquarium**

1. How do the first three lines of the poem encourage you to think about creatures in a new way? Make a list of the other **images** in the poem that continue the **personification** suggested by a "frog who works out / in the clean gym" (lines 1–2).

2. Why do you think Willard ends the poem with a question, and what does her question tell you about the **speaker's** attitude toward frogs?

**SEE ACTIVITIES, PAGE 104.**

# THE SECOND DIMENSION: JOURNEYS

PHOTO BY LINDSAY GREENE

## Patrick Ewing Takes a Foul Shot[1]

Diane Ackerman (1948– )

Ewing sweating,
molding the ball
with spidery hands,
packing it, packing it,
into a snowball's
chance of a goal,
rolling his shoulders
through a silent earthquake,
rocking from one foot
to the other, sweating,
bouncing it, oh, sweet
honey, molding it,
packing it tight,
he fires:

floats it up on one palm
as if surfacing
from the clear green Caribbean[2]
with a shell
whose roar wraps around him,
whose surf breaks
deep into his arena
where light and time
and pupils[3] jump
because he jumps

1985

1 Patrick Ewing — a famous basketball player for the New York Knickerbockers, who was traded in the year 2000 to the Seattle Supersonics. Originally from Jamaica, Ewing is known for his unusually large hands and his high free throw (foul shot) record. A foul shot is a throw from the foul line given to a player after a foul has been called on an opponent.

2 Caribbean — a sea in the North Atlantic Ocean bounded by the coasts of Central America, South America, and the West Indies. The extended simile is especially significant because of Ewing's Caribbean origins.

3 pupils — the black opening in the iris of the eye that opens and contracts to allow light to pass to the retina.

## Questions for **Patrick Ewing Takes a Foul Shot**

1. Circle the nouns and verbs that are often used at a basketball game. Notice the poem's punctuation. Why do you think the poet chose to write her poem in one long sentence?

2. List the **metaphors** in the first stanza. What do they tell you about Ewing and the basketball? In the second stanza, after Ewing "fires" (line 14) his shot, which words create an **extended simile** describing the ball's flight in the arena? Place brackets around the parts of the extended simile in the second stanza. What do the words enable you to see, hear, and feel about this dramatic moment in the game?

**SEE ACTIVITIES, PAGE 105.**

# Little Clown, My Heart

Sandra Cisneros (1954– )

Little clown, my heart,
Spangled again and lopsided,
Handstands and Peking pirouettes,[1]
Backflips snapping open like
A carpenter's hinged ruler,

Little gimp-footed hurray,[2]
Paper parasol of pleasures,
Fleshy undertongue[3] of sorrows,
Sweet potato plant of my addictions,

Acapulco cliff-diver *corazón*,[4]
Fine as an obsidian dagger,[5]
Alley-oop[6] and here we go
Into the froth, my life,
Into the flames!

1994

---

1 Peking pirouettes — a movement of acrobats and dancers such as those associated with the Peking circus (from Beijing, China). In ballet, a pirouette is a full turn of the body on the tip of the toe or on the ball of the foot.

2 gimp-footed hurray — *gimp* is slang for someone who limps.

3 undertongue — a play on the word *undertone*, meaning a tone of low pitch or volume.

4 Acapulco cliff-diver *corazón* — a reference to the divers made famous by their dangerous high dives from the cliffs of Acapulco, Mexico, into the Pacific Ocean. *Corazón* is Spanish for *heart*.

5 obsidian dagger — a dagger made of obsidian, a black volcanic glass frequently used for tools in the Stone Age.

6 Alley-oop — slang for *turn upside down*.

## Questions for **Little Clown, My Heart**

1. Make a list of the poem's words and phrases that are associated with clowns or circuses. What do these words tell you about the **speaker's** "heart," to which she refers as "little clown" in the first line?

2. Look at the last three lines of the poem. What do "froth" (line 13) and "flames" (line 14) tell you about the contrasts in the **speaker's** feelings? Why do you think the speaker says "Alley-oop and here we go" (line 12)?

**SEE ACTIVITIES, PAGE 105.**

## The Base Stealer

Robert Francis (1901–1987)

Poised between going on and back, pulled
Both ways taut like a tightrope-walker,
Fingertips pointing the opposites,
Now bouncing tiptoe like a dropped ball
Or a kid skipping rope, come on, come on,
Running like a scattering of steps sidewise.
How he teeters, skitters, tingles, teases,
Taunts them, hovers like an ecstatic bird.
He's only flirting, crowd him, crowd him,
Delicate, delicate, delicate, delicate—now!

1948

## Questions for **The Base Stealer**

1. What is the **context** of the poem suggested by the title and the first line? What comparisons can you find in the poem between the action of stealing a base in baseball and other familiar activities? (The word "like" in lines 2, 4, 6, and 8 should help you find at least four suggested comparisons, or **similes**.)

2. Why does the **speaker** change from his command "crowd him, crowd him" to "delicate, delicate, delicate, delicate" in the last two lines of the poem? What does the change enable you to picture in the scene?

**SEE ACTIVITIES, PAGE 105.**

## Where There's a Wall

Joy Kogawa (1935– )

Where there's a wall
there's a way through a
gate or a door. There's even
a ladder perhaps and a
sentinel who sometimes sleeps.
There are secret passwords you
can overhear. There are methods
of torture for extracting clues
to maps of underground passages.
There are zeppelins, helicopters,
rockets, bombs, battering rams,
armies with trumpets whose
all at once blast shatters
the foundations.

Where there's a wall there are
words to whisper by loose bricks,
wailing prayers[1] to utter, birds
to carry messages taped to their feet.
There are letters to be written—
poems even.

Faint as in a dream
is the voice that calls
from the belly
of the wall.

1985

---

1 wailing prayers — a reference to the Wailing Wall in the old city of Jerusalem, a sacred place of Jewish worship where people often slip papers with prayers into the cracks between the stones of the wall.

## Questions for **Where There's a Wall**

1. What are your personal associations with the word *wall* or the concept of walls in general? What are the functions of walls, and what do you know about their role in history? Which of the poem's historical references, if any, are familiar to you?

2. Make a list of the words in the first **stanza** that are associated with ways of getting over, under, or through a wall. With what events are words like "sentinel," "torture," "bombs," and "battering rams" connected? How do these words and their associations differ from the **images** in the second and third stanzas? What does the author want us to understand about the importance of walls in our lives?

**SEE ACTIVITIES, PAGE 105.**

## Sky Diver

Adrien Stoutenberg (1916–1982)

Grotesque, jumping out
like a clothed frog, helmet and glasses,
arms and legs wading the sky,
feet flapping before the cloth flower opens;
then suspended, poised,
an exclamation point upside-down,
and going down, swaying over corn and creeks
and highways scribbled
over the bones of fish and eagles.

There is the interim between air and earth,
time to study steeples
and the underwings of birds going over,
before the unseen chasm,
the sudden jaw open and hissing.

Lying here after the last jump
I see how fanatic roots are,
how moles breathe through darkness,
how deep the earth can be.

1968

## Questions for **Sky Diver**

1. Next to each **stanza** in the space to the right of the poem, label the stage of sky diving that is described. Then underline the key **images** or **figures of speech** that help you visualize each stage.

2. At the end of the sky-diving experience, why does the **speaker** say "I see how fanatic roots are . . . how deep the earth can be" (lines 16–18)? To what physical force and instinct is he referring?

**SEE ACTIVITIES, PAGE 105.**

## The Great Figure

### William Carlos Williams (1883–1963)

Among the rain
and lights
I saw the figure 5[1]
in gold
on a red
firetruck
moving
tense
unheeded
to gong clangs
siren howls
and wheels rumbling
through the dark city.

1921

---

1 figure 5 — reference to the figure 5 on the side of a moving fire engine. The image of "the figure 5" in Williams's poem inspired American painter Charles Demuth in 1928 to create a painting that was considered "a visual equivalent to his friend William Carlos Williams's image of a fire-truck roaring down a Manhattan street" and includes references to Williams, "whose name appears in various guises and combinations on the canvas" (from Robert Hughes, *The Shock of the Future*, Knopf, 1991, p. 330).

## Questions for **The Great Figure**

1. This poem focuses on a single **image** in a single sentence. Underline the words and phrases that enable you to see and hear the scene being described. Which words or images enable you to visualize the scene in motion (using **kinesthetic imagery**), as if it were a film?

2. What contrasts does the **speaker** notice between "The Great Figure" (title) and the "red / firetruck" (lines 5–6) and between "The Great Figure" and "the dark city" (line 13)? What is the significance of the contrast?

**SEE ACTIVITIES, PAGE 105.**

## Life's Work

### Maxine Kumin (1925– )

Mother my good girl
I remember this old story:
you fresh out of the Conservatory
at eighteen a Bach[1] specialist
in a starched shirtwaist[2]
begging permission to go on tour
with the nimble violinist you were
never to accompany and he
flinging his music down
the rosin[3] from his bow
flaking line by line
like grace notes[4] on the treble clef
and my grandfather
that estimable man I never met
scrubbing your mouth with a handkerchief
saying no daughter of mine
tearing loose the gold locket
you wore with no one's picture in it
and the whole German house on 15th street
at righteous whiteheat . . . .

At eighteen I chose to be a swimmer.
My long hair dripped through dinner
onto the china plate.
My fingers wrinkled like Sunsweet[5]
yellow raisins from the afternoon workout.
My mouth chewed but I was doing laps.
I entered the water like a knife.
I was all muscle and seven[6] doors.
A frog on the turning board.[7]
King of the Eels and the Eel's wife.[8]
I swallowed and prayed
to be allowed to join the Aquacade[9]
and my perfect daddy
who carried you off to elope
after the fingerboard[10] snapped
and the violinist lost his case
my daddy wearing gravy on his face
swore on the carrots and the boiled beef
that I would come to nothing
that I would come to grief . . . .

Well, the firm old fathers are dead
and I didn't come to grief.[11]
I came to words instead
to tell the little tale that's left:
the midnights of my childhood still go on
the stairs speak again under your foot
the heavy parlor door folds shut
and "Au Clair de la Lune"[12]
puckers from the obedient keys
plain as a schoolroom clock ticking
and what I hear more clearly than Debussy's[13]
lovesong is the dry aftersound
of your long nails clicking.

1975

---

1 Bach — Johann Sebastian Bach (1685-1750), a German composer.

2 shirtwaist — a belted dress, the top of which is tailored like a shirt.

3 rosin — powder made from tree resin and rubbed on the bow of a stringed instrument such as a violin to increase the bow's sliding friction.

4 grace notes — short notes that embellish or ornament the melody and are not part of the harmonic structure.

5 Sunsweet — a company that packages raisins.

6 seven — a mystic, sacred number that is the sum of three and four, both considered to be lucky numbers in ancient Babylonian, Egyptian, and Hebrew cultures.

7 frog on the turning board — turning board is presumably a play on the word *diving board*; frogs are known for their ability to jump great distances.

8 King of Eels and the Eel's wife — eels are snake-like fish known for their slipperiness and speed in the water. This line suggests that the speaker would like her swimming skills to be equal to those of the leaders of the eels.

9 Aquacade — an exhibition of diving and swimming, usually accompanied by music.

10 fingerboard — the strip of wood on the neck of a stringed instrument such as a violin or cello, against which the strings are stopped by the fingers.

11 come to grief — a phrase no longer used very often which means to "turn out badly."

12 "Au Clair de la Lune"— a romantic piece composed by Claude Debussy, a French composer who lived from 1862-1918.

13 Claude Debussy — French composer of "Au Clair de la Lune" who lived from 1862–1918.

## Questions for **Life's Work**

1. What problem or obstacles do the **speaker** and her mother have in common? Underline phrases that reveal their determination to overcome their respective fathers' predictions about them. What details can you find in the poem to show that the phrase "the firm old fathers" (line 41) is meant to be **ironic**?

2. Circle the **metaphors** and **similes** in the poem. Why are they effective?

**SEE ACTIVITIES, PAGE 105.**

## Liddy's Orange

### Sharon Olds (1942– )

The rind lies on the table where Liddy has left it
torn into pieces the size of petals and
curved like petals, rayed out like a
full-blown rose, one touch will make it come apart.
The lining of the rind is wet and chalky as
Devonshire cream,[1] rich as the glaucous
lining of a boiled egg, all that protein
cupped in the ripped shell. And the navel,
torn out carefully,
lies there like a fat gold
bouquet, and the scar of the stem, picked out
with her nails, and still attached to the white
thorn of the central integument,
lies on the careful heap, a tool laid
down at the end of a ceremony.
All here speaks of ceremony,
the sheen of the acrid juice, which is all that is
left of the flesh, the pieces lying in
profound order like natural order,
as if this simply happened, the way her
life at 13 looks like something that's just
happening, unless you see her
standing over it, delicately clawing it open.

1987

---

1 Devonshire cream — thick, rich cream from Devon, England, often served with jam and scones (a British term for biscuits).

## Questions for **Liddy's Orange**

1. Circle or underline words and phrases used to describe the orange. To what senses do they appeal? Why do you think the poet uses a comparison between an orange and a flower in a poem about an adolescent (see title and lines 2–3)?

2. What **extended metaphor** is central to the way the **speaker** feels about her daughter? Discuss the meaning of lines 16 through 23.

**SEE ACTIVITIES, PAGE 105.**

# The Waking

Theodore Roethke (1908–1963)

I wake to sleep, and take my waking slow.
I feel my fate in what I cannot fear.
I learn by going where I have to go.

We think by feeling. What is there to know?
I hear my being dance from ear to ear.
I wake to sleep, and take my waking slow.

Of those so close beside me, which are you?
God bless the Ground! I shall walk softly there,
And learn by going where I have to go,

Light takes the Tree; but who can tell us how?
The lowly worm climbs up a winding stair;
I wake to sleep, and take my waking slow.

Great Nature has another thing to do
To you and me; so take the lively air,
And, lovely, learn by going where to go.

This shaking keeps me steady. I should know.
What falls away is always. And is near.
I wake to sleep, and take my waking slow.
I learn by going where I have to go.

1953

## Questions for **The Waking**

1. Underline the poem's three questions. What important aspects of a person's life do they address? Why are these important questions in anyone's life?

2. Look up **paradox** in the glossary. Explain why the following statements are paradoxes: "I wake to sleep" (line 1), "We think by feeling" (line 4), "This shaking keeps me steady" (line 16), and "What falls away is always. And is near" (line 17). Look for clues in the poem that help you interpret what the **speaker** means by each paradox. How do the paradoxes lead you to find more than one meaning for the poem's title?

**SEE ACTIVITIES, PAGE 105.**

# Black Hair

## Gary Soto (1952– )

At eight I was brilliant with my body.
In July, that ring of heat
We all jumped through, I sat in the bleachers
Of Romain Playground,[1] in the lengthening
Shade that rose from our dirty feet.
The game before us was more than baseball.
It was a figure—Hector Moreno
Quick and hard with turned muscles,
His crouch the one I assumed before an altar
Of worn baseball cards, in my room.

I came here because I was Mexican, a stick
Of brown light in love with those
Who could do it—the triple[2] and hard slide,[3]
The gloves eating balls into double plays.[4]
What could I do with fifty pounds, my shyness,
My black torch of hair, about to go out?
Father was dead, his face no longer
Hanging over the table or our sleep,
And mother was the terror of mouths
Twisting hurt by butter knives.

In the bleachers I was brilliant with my body,
Waving players in and stomping with my feet,
Growing sweaty in the presence of white shirts.
I chewed sunflower seeds. I drank water
And bit my arm through the late innings.
When Hector lined balls[5] into deep
Center, in my mind I rounded the bases
With him, my face flared, my hair lifting
Beautifully, because we were coming home
To the arms of brown people.

1985

---

1 Romain Playground — a playground outside Gary Soto's childhood home in Fresno, California, where he and his brother played baseball for the Little League.

2 triple – a play during which the batter succeeds in getting to third base.

3 hard slide — a forceful slide into a base.

4 double play — a situation in which there are two outs in one play.

5 lined balls — hit balls in a straight line.

## Questions for **Black Hair**

1. For what reasons does the **speaker** enjoy the baseball game? Underline phrases in the poem that reveal his feelings about himself when he is in the bleachers. Why is the title of the poem important?

2. What do we learn about the **speaker's** family in lines 17–20? How does the speaker's experience of the game contrast with his life at home? Circle **images** that show that contrast.

## How Everything Happens (Based on a study of the Wave)

May Swenson (1919–1989)

happen.
to
up
stacking
is
something
When nothing is happening

When it happens
something
pulls
back
not
to
happen.

When has happened.
pulling back stacking up
happens

has happened stacks up.
When it something nothing
pulls back while

Then nothing is happening.

happens.
and
forward
pushes
up
stacks
something
Then

1970

## Questions for **How Everything Happens**

1. How does the **shape** of "How Everything Happens" create a picture of the sequence and pacing of a wave's motions and about events in time?

2. How does the poet's use of **repetition** and experimentation with **shape** reinforce the idea of action and reaction described in the poem? What examples of action and reaction can you think of in your own life?

**SEE ACTIVITIES, PAGE 105.**

# THE THIRD DIMENSION: RELATIONSHIPS

PHOTO BY ABE NACHBAUR

## Sunday Night at Grandfather's

Rita Dove (1952– )

He likes to joke and all of his jokes were practical.
The bent thumb jiggling between two ribs, his
Faked and drunken swoon. We tipped by and
He caught us, grandfather's right, right
Up to the cliff of his pure white
Shirt, real Fruit-of-the-
Loom.[1] We shrieked and
He cackled like
A living
Ghost.

He hated Billy the parakeet, mean as half-baked sin.
He hated church-going women and the radio turned
Up loud. His favorite son, called Billy
Too, had flown the coop[2] although
Each year he visited, each
Time from a different
City, gold
Tooth and
Drunk.

Then out came the cherry soda and potato chips and pretzels.
Grandma humming hymns and rocking in the back bedroom.
Dad holding Billy out on a thick and bitten finger,
Saying *Here: Come on Joe—touch him.*
Every Sunday night the same.
Dad's quiet urging and
That laugh: *You've*
*Got to be*
*Kidding,*
*Son.*

1993

1 Fruit-of-the-Loom — the name of a company that manufactures shirts and underwear.

2 flown the coop — a slang expression for having left; taken off.

## Questions for **Sunday Night at Grandfather's**

1. Circle words and phrases that describe the grandfather. What kind of person is he? Do you like him? What attitude does the **speaker** reveal toward the grandfather?

2. The parakeet and the "favorite son" (line 13) are both called Billy. What else do they have in common? Why is the **image** of "flown the coop" (line 14) appropriate for Billy the son? Explain the images in lines 22–29. How could they apply to Billy, the son, as well as the bird?

**SEE ACTIVITIES, PAGE 106.**

## Parents' Pantoum

Carolyn Kizer (1925– )

Where did these enormous children come from,
More ladylike than we have ever been?
Some of ours look older than we feel.
How did they appear in their long dresses

More ladylike than we have ever been?
But they moan about their aging more than we do,
In their fragile heels and long black dresses.
Then say they admire our youthful spontaneity.

They moan about their aging more than we do,
A somber group—why don't they brighten up?
Though they say they admire our youthful spontaneity
They beg us to be dignified like them

As they ignore our pleas to brighten up.
Someday perhaps we'll capture their attention,
Then we won't try to be dignified like them
Nor they to be so gently patronizing.

Someday perhaps we'll capture their attention.
Don't they know that we're supposed to be the stars?
Instead they are so gently patronizing.
It makes us feel like children—second-childish?

Perhaps we're too accustomed to be stars,
The famous flowers glowing in the garden,
So now we pout like children. Second-childish?
Quaint fragments of forgotten history?

Our daughters stroll together in the garden,
Chatting of news we've chosen to ignore,
Pausing to toss us morsels of their history,
Not questions to which only we know answers.

Eyes closed to news we've chosen to ignore,
We'd rather excavate old memories,
Disdaining age, ignoring pain, avoiding mirrors.
Why do they never listen to our stories?

Because they hate to excavate old memories
They don't believe our stories have an end.
They don't ask questions because they dread the answers.
They don't see that we've become their mirrors,

We offspring of our enormous children.

For Maxine Kumin

1996

## Questions for **Parents' Pantoum**

1. What do you think the **speaker** means by "enormous children" (lines 1 and 37)? Underline other words and phrases she uses to describe her children and those of the friend she is addressing. What feelings toward the children do these words and phrases express? Now circle words and phrases that refer to the children's views of their mothers. How do the children feel about their mothers?

2. Look up **pantoum** in **Classic Models,** page 98. How does the repetition of lines in the pantoum form add to your understanding of the poem's **theme** of change in mother/daughter relationships?

SEE ACTIVITIES, PAGE 106.

# Whose Mouth Do I Speak With

Suzanne Rancourt

I can remember my father bringing home spruce gum.[1]
He worked in the woods and filled his pockets
with golden chunks of pitch.
For his children
he provided this special sacrament
and we'd gather at his feet, around his legs,
bumping his lunchbox, and his empty thermos rattle inside.
Our skin would stick to Daddy's gluey clothing
and we'd smell like Mumma's Pine Sol.[2]
We had no money for storebought gum
but that's all right.
The spruce gum
was so close to chewing amber[3]
as though in our mouths we held the eyes of Coyote
and how many other children had fathers
that placed on their innocent, anxious tongues
the blood of trees?

1994

---

1 spruce gum — sap from a spruce tree.

2 Pine Sol — the brand name of a liquid used for cleaning.

3 amber — a reddish or brownish fossil substance obtained from certain pine trees, such as spruces, and often polished and used as jewelry.

## Questions for **Whose Mouth Do I Speak With**

1. Underline **images** in the poem that appeal to the senses. How do these phrases emphasize the importance of the children's experience?

2. Why do you think the **speaker** describes the experience of chewing spruce gum as "so close to chewing amber / as though in our mouths we held the eyes of Coyote" (lines 13–14)? Why are the children's tongues described as "innocent, anxious" (line 16)? How do these lines relate to the meaning of the title and its reference to speaking?

**SEE ACTIVITIES, PAGE 106.**

# Ballad of Birmingham[1]

*(On the Bombing of a Church in Birmingham, Alabama, 1963)*

Dudley Randall (1914–2000)

"Mother dear, may I go downtown
Instead of out to play.
And march the streets of Birmingham
In a Freedom March today?"

"No, baby, no, you may not go,
For the dogs are fierce and wild,
And clubs and hoses, guns and jail
Aren't good for a little child."

"But, mother, I won't be alone.
Other children will go with me
And march the streets of Birmingham
To make our country free."

"No, baby, no, you may not go,
For I fear the guns will fire.
But you may go to church instead
And sing in the children's choir."

She has combed and brushed her night-dark hair,
And bathed rose petal sweet,
And drawn white gloves on her small brown hands,
And white shoes on her feet.

Her mother smiled to know her child
Was in the sacred place,
But that smile was the last smile
To come upon her face.

For when she heard the explosion,
Her eyes grew wet and wild.
She raced through the streets of Birmingham
Calling for her child.

She clawed through bits of glass and brick
Then lifted out a shoe.
"O here's the shoe my baby wore
But, baby, where are you?"

1 — On September 15, 1963, a bomb exploded during church services at the Sixteenth Street Baptist Church in Birmingham, Alabama. Four young girls, Addie Collins, Carole Robertson, Cynthia Wesley, and Denise McNair, were in the changing room in the basement. They were killed and twenty others were seriously injured. Local FBI agents recommended charging at least four suspects with the bombing, but FBI director J. Edgar Hoover blocked the prosecution. One suspect, Robert Edward Chambliss, was convicted 14 years after the murders. He died in prison without admitting any role in the bombing. In 1980 a second suspect, dying of cancer, admitted he helped set the bomb. On May 17, 2001, former Ku Klux Klan members Thomas Blanton Jr. and Bobby Frank Cherry were indicted by an Alabama grand jury on murder charges in connection with the bombing. Thomas Blanton was sentenced to life imprisonment on May 1, 2001.

## Questions for **Ballad of Birmingham**

1. Read about the **ballad** in the **Classic Models** section of the book. How does the poet use the ballad form in this modern poem to express powerful feelings about racial conflicts in the United States at the beginning of the Civil Rights Movement (1960s)?

2. What **irony** is evident in the mother's decision to send her child to church?

**SEE ACTIVITIES, PAGE 106.**

## Listening to Grownups Quarreling,

Ruth Whitman (1922–1999)

standing in the hall against the
wall with my little brother, blown
like leaves against the wall by their
voices, my head like a pingpong ball
between the paddles of their anger;
I knew what it meant
to tremble like a leaf.

Cold with their wrath, I heard
the claws of the rain
pounce. Floods
poured through the city,
skies clapped over me,
and I was shaken, shaken
like a mouse
between their jaws.

1968

## Questions for **Listening to Grownups Quarreling,**

1. Underline the **similes** and examples of **personification** in the poem. How do these **figures of speech** emphasize the emotions felt by the **speaker**?

2. Find examples of **alliteration** and **assonance** throughout the poem. Why is the repetition of these particular sounds appropriate in expressing how the speaker feels? What is the effect of repeating the word "shaken" in line 13?

**SEE ACTIVITIES, PAGE 106.**

## Son

Al Young (1939– )

You should hammer on him to clean
his undersea room? You should stay
on his back or up in his chest
until he picks the clothes
up off the floor, unglues old gum
and fudge and snot and pizza sauce
from chairs and shelves, and drags
the mildewed bathing suit and towel
from under his bed, until he sweeps
and dusts? What for? What drawer
should you pull out to prove
your power over him? The lesson
when you were going to school back home
was this: At 13 you do your best
to let your loathesome parents know
they're not the ones who run your show.

A little well-staged chaos is in order.

1990

## Questions for **Son**

1. Who is the "you" in lines 1 – 13? How does the identity of "you" change in line 14? How does the **speaker's** use of questions affect the tone of the poem?

2. From whose **point of view** are the parents described as "loathesome" (line 15)? Why?

**SEE ACTIVITIES, PAGE 106.**

## The Immigrant

Eric Chock (1950– )

they knew
she was naturally dark
under the working tan[1]
they knew
thick eyebrows were grown
to shade the sun
or catch the sweat
as with gloves and hoe
clearing land
she worked
her body
they said was made
for a field

under the brim
of her hat
her eyes stared at the ground
like two lost stones
after rain

she stands
a curved stem in the wind
over those rows of thin leaves
she keeps the corners of the hoe
chipping the unwanted green from the field
and as she works toward the tool shack
leaning on the horizon
she sees in its corrugated roof and wooden walls
the ship of her dreams
holding sky

weed by weed she pulls her way
each stroke of the hoe
notching the earth ocean
waiting for when she can walk
the rest of her life
into the cool rectangular boat
and sail across those cool latitudes
eating lunch at the window
as whole nations pass by.

1990

1 working tan — a play on the common phrase "I'm working on a tan," associated with people who purposely seek a suntan during their leisure time. The "working tan" of the woman in the poem, however, results from her outdoor manual work.

## Questions for **The Immigrant**

1. To whom does the first word of the poem, "they," refer? What attitudes toward the immigrant are revealed in the physical description of the woman working in the fields?

2. How does the **extended metaphor** of "ship of her dreams" (line 27) help you to look at the woman differently from the way "they" (line 1) see her?

**SEE ACTIVITIES, PAGE 107.**

## jackie robinson[1]

### Lucille Clifton (1936– )

ran against walls
without breaking.
in night games
was not foul
but, brave as a hit
over whitestone fences,
entered the conquering dark.

1990

---

1 Jackie Robinson — (1919–1972) the first African American to play in the major baseball leagues in the twentieth century.

## Questions for **jackie robinson**

1. What do the lines "ran against walls / without breaking" (1–2) and "was not foul / but brave as a hit" (lines 4–5) tell you about Jackie Robinson? How does the **speaker** regard him?

2. Jackie Robinson was a famous African American athlete. What words and **images** suggest that he has succeeded in a world that is not always sympathetic or willing to break with tradition?

**SEE ACTIVITIES, PAGE 107.**

## Frederick Douglass[1]

### Robert Hayden (1913– )

When it is finally ours, this freedom, this liberty, this beautiful
and terrible thing, needful to man as air,
usable as earth; when it belongs at last to all,
when it is truly instinct, brain matter, diastole, systole,
reflex action; when it is finally won; when it is more
than the gaudy mumbo jumbo[2] of politicians:
this man, this Douglass, this former slave, this Negro
beaten to his knees, exiled, visioning a world
where none is lonely, none hunted, alien,
this man, superb in love and logic, this man
shall be remembered. Oh, not with statues' rhetoric,
not with legends and poems and wreaths of bronze alone,
but with the lives grown out of his life, the lives
fleshing his dream of the beautiful, needful thing.

1985

---

1 Frederick Douglass — (1817–1895) an African American who worked to end the practice of slavery. His published autobiography, *The Life and Times of Frederick Douglass* (1845), challenged the stereotype of a slave.

2 mumbo jumbo — meaningless or senseless language, usually meant to confuse the listener.

## Questions for **Frederick Douglass**

1. Why do you think the **speaker** describes freedom as both "beautiful" (line 1) and "terrible" (line 2)?

2. What facts do you learn about Frederick Douglass's life in lines 7–10? According to the **speaker,** how will Douglass be remembered? Which **images** in lines 11–14 convey that idea?

**SEE ACTIVITIES, PAGE 107.**

# What For

## Garrett Hongo (1950– )

At six I lived for spells:
how a few Hawaiian words could call
up the rain, could hymn like the sea
in the long swirl of chambers
curling in the nautilus of a shell,
how Amida's[1] ballads of the Buddhaland[2]
in the drone of the priest's liturgy
could conjure money from the poor
and give them nothing but mantras,[3]
and strange syllables that healed desire.

I lived for stories about the war
my grandfather told over *hana*[4] cards
slapping them down on the mats
with a sharp Japanese *kiai*.[5]

I lived for the songs my grandmother sang
stirring curry into a thick stew,
weaving a calligraphy of Kannon's[6] love
into grass mats and straw sandals.

I lived for the red volcano dirt
staining my toes, the salt residue
of surf and sea wind in my hair,
the arc of a flat stone skipping
in the hollow trough of a wave.

I lived a child's world, waited
for my father to drag himself home,
dusted with blasts of sand, powdered rock,
and the strange ash of raw cement,
his deafness made worse by the clang
of pneumatic[7] drills, sore in his bones
from the buckings of a jackhammer.[8]
He'd hand me a scarred lunchpail
let me unlace the hightop G.I.[9] boots,
call him the new name I'd invented
that day in school, write it for him
on his newspaper. He'd rub my face
with hands that felt like gravel roads,
tell me to move, go play, and then he'd
walk to the laundry sink to scrub,
rinse the dirt of his long day
from a face brown and grained as koa[10] wood.

I wanted to take away the pain
in his legs, the swelling in his joints,
give him back his hearing,
clear and rare as crystal chimes,
the fins of glass that wrinkled
and sparked the air with their sound.

I wanted to heal the sores that work
and war had sent to him,
let him play catch in the backyard
with me, tossing a tennis ball
past papaya trees without the shoulders
of pain shrugging back his arms.

I wanted to become a doctor of pure magic,
to string a necklace of sweet words
fragrant as pine needles and plumeria,[11]
fragrant as the bread my mother baked,
place it like a lei[12] of cowrie[13] bells
and *pikake*[14] flowers around my father's neck,
and chant him a blessing, a sutra.[15]

1 Amida — a name for Buddha (566–480 B.C.), an Indian religious leader who founded Buddhism.

2 Buddhaland — any place in which Buddhism is practiced.

3 mantras — words or formulas to be recited or sung.

4 hana — a brief statement of Buddhist wisdom.

5 kiai — a martial arts term for a forceful gesture accompanied by a shout or loud exclamation.

6 Kannon — in Buddhism, "He Who Perceives the Sounds of the World." An enlightened soul who attends Buddha and is able to take on various forms to save human beings. He/she is a being between a god and a human.

7 pneumatic drill — a drill operated by air pressure and used for such jobs as digging up asphalt.

8 jackhammer — a portable rock drill operated with compressed air.

9 G.I. — initials for "general issue" referring to clothing or equipment of a style or type used by the United States army.

10 koa — a dark, rare wood.

11 plumeria — a tropical tree with large fragrant flowers that are white, yellow, or purple.

12 lei — a wreath of flowers or leaves.

13 cowrie — a type of mollusk whose shells are made into necklaces.

14 pikake — small, white, fragrant flowers often used in leis.

15 sutra — a sermon of Buddha.

## Questions for **What For**

1. Underline phrases that describe the experiences the **speaker** enjoyed as a child. Then list phrases that describe the father's life. How do the experiences of the speaker contrast with those of his father? Why do you think Hongo chose the title "What For"?

2. Make a list of **similes** and **metaphors** and discuss how they contribute to the experiences that the **speaker** describes.

**SEE ACTIVITIES, PAGE 107.**

## Blue Lantern

Cathy Song (1955– )

The blue lantern light
was like a full moon
swelling above the hush
of the mock orange shrubs
that separated our houses.

It was light
from your grandfather's room.

I remember the music
at night.

I dreamed the music
came in squares,
like birthday chocolate,
through a window
on a blue plate.

From his shakuhachi,[1]
shavings of notes,
floated, and fell;
melted where the stillness
inserted itself back into the night.
It was quiet then until dawn,
broken once by a single wailing:
the sound of an animal
whose hind leg is caught in a trap.
It was your grandfather
mourning his dead wife.
He played for her each night;
her absence,
the shape of his grief
funneled through the bamboo flute.
A ritual of remembrance,
keeping her memory alive
with his old breath.
He played unknowingly
to the child next door
who lay stricken by the music
transposed to her body,
waiting for the cry
that always surprised her;
like a glimpse of shadow
darting through the room
before she would drift off to sleep.

I knew you were in the room
just beyond the music.

1983

---

1 shakuhachi — a Japanese bamboo flute.

## Questions for **Blue Lantern**

1. The **speaker** is addressing a child whose grandfather played music that deeply affected the speaker in her past. Find examples in the poem of **figures of speech** associated with light, dark, and sound. What feelings do the figures of speech convey about the speaker's memory of the grandfather and the importance of his music to the child? What do the figures of speech convey about the relationship between the grandfather and his dead wife?

2. What does the reference to "a single wailing" (line 21) and the **image** of "an animal / whose hind leg is caught in a trap" (lines 22–23) tell you about the grandfather's feelings? Explain the title.

**SEE ACTIVITIES, PAGE 107.**

## Matmiya[1]

### Mary TallMountain (1918–1994)

*for my grandmother*

I see you sitting
Implanted by roots
Coiled deep from your thighs.
Roots, flesh red, centuries pale.
Hairsprings[2] wound tight.
Through fertile earthscapes
Where each layer feeds the next
Into depths immutable.

Though you must rise, must
Move large and slow
When it is time, O my
Gnarled mother-vine, ancient
As vanished ages,
Your spirit remains
Nourished,
Nourishing me.

I see your figure wrapped in skins
Curved into a mound of earth
Holding your rich dark roots.
Matmiya,
I see you sitting.

---

1 Matmiya — a Native American word meaning mountain.

2 hairsprings — spiral-shaped springs that swing back and forth to regulate the balance of a timepiece.

## Questions for **Matmiya**

1. What qualities of the grandmother do the following words and phrases suggest: "Implanted by roots" (line 2), "Coiled" (line 3), "Through fertile earthscapes / Where each layer feeds the next" (lines 6–7), and "Gnarled mother-vine" (line 12)? Why are the roots both "flesh red" and "centuries pale" (line 4)? To what is the grandmother being compared?

2. Circle the **images** that convey how the **speaker** feels toward her grandmother. Why are they effective images?

**SEE ACTIVITIES, PAGE 107.**

# CLOSE-UPS OF TWO POETS: POEMS AND QUESTIONS

## EMILY DICKINSON

AMHERST COLLEGE ARCHIVES
AND SPECIAL COLLECTIONS

**Emily Dickinson** (1830–1886) was born in Amherst, Massachusetts, where she lived in relative seclusion after studying at the local academy and Mount Holyoke Seminary. Her relationships were intellectual, and she exchanged letters on literary topics with a few close friends who were also mentors. Although only six of her poems were published during her lifetime, a collection of 1,147 poems published after Dickinson's death were acclaimed by critics and scholars. Lacking titles, the poems are numbered in the order in which Dickinson gathered them. Dickinson's poems are known for their conciseness, sharp imagery, playful humor, and experimental sound devices and punctuation. A keen observer, she captures the idiosyncrasies of the natural world, the strange inventions of the industrial revolution, and the contradictions and complexities in human emotions.

# YUSEF KOMUNYAKAA

DON GETSUG

Born in Bogalusa, Louisiana, **Yusef Komunyakaa** (1947– ) has written numerous books of poetry including *Thieves of Paradise*, a finalist for the National Book Critics Award; *Neon Vernacular: New and Selected Poems 1977–1989*, winner of the Pulitzer Prize and the Kingsley Tufts Poetry Award; and *I Apologize for the Eyes in My Head*, winner of the San Francisco Poetry Center Award. His prose is collected in *Blues Notes: Essays, Interviews & Commentaries.* Komunyakaa has received many honors, including the William Faulkner Prize from the Université de Rennes, the Thomas Forcade Award, the Hanes Poetry Prize, several fellowships, and the Bronze Star for his service in Vietnam, where he was a correspondent and managing editor of the *Southern Cross*. Komunyakaa is Professor in the Council of Humanities and Creative Writing Program at Princeton University and a recently elected Chancellor of the Academy of American Poets. He lives in New York City.

## 585

I like to see it lap the Miles—
And lick the Valleys up—
And stop to feed itself at Tanks—
And then—prodigious step

Around a Pile of Mountains—
And supercilious peer
In Shanties—by the sides of Roads—
And then a Quarry pare

To fit its Ribs
And crawl between
Complaining all the while
In horrid—hooting stanza—
Then chase itself down Hill—

And neigh like Boanerges[1]
Then—punctual as a Star
Stop—docile and omnipotent
At its own stable door—

1862

1 Boanerges — a reference to the "sons of thunder" in the New Testament of the Bible (Mark 3:17), specifically John and James, two of the twelve apostles appointed by Jesus "to be sent out to preach and have authority to cast out demons" (Mark 3: 14-15).

## Questions for **585**

1. Circle the words in the poem that provide clues to the identity of the poem's subject, the "it" (line 1) that can "lap the Miles" (line 1). Then underline the words and phrases in the poem that create an **extended metaphor** comparing the poem's subject with an animal. What do these **images** and comparisons reveal about the **speaker's** attitude toward the subject? What is the subject and to which animal is the subject compared?

2. Find examples of the poem's use of various **sound devices** such as **alliteration**, **consonance**, and **assonance**. How do these sound devices help you hear as well as see the subject of the poem?

**SEE ACTIVITIES, PAGE 108.**

## 605

The Spider holds a Silver Ball
In unperceived Hands—
And dancing softly to Himself
His yarn of Pearl—unwinds—

He plies from Nought to Nought—
In unsubstantial Trade—
Supplants our Tapestries with His—
In half the period—

An Hour to rear supreme
His Continents of Light—
Then dangle from the Housewife's Broom—
His Boundaries—forgot—

1862

## Questions on **605**

1. Circle the verbs in the poem that are associated with the "Spider" (line 1). What do they tell you about the spider's activities?

2. What is the effect on your view of the spider of such **images** as "Silver Ball" (line 1), "unperceived Hands" (line 2), "unsubstantial Trade" (line 6), and "His Continents of Light" (line 10)? How do those images of the spider compare with the description of the spider's fate in the last two lines of the poem: "Then dangle from the Housewife's Broom— / His Boundaries—forgot— (lines 11–12)?

**SEE ACTIVITIES, PAGE 108.**

## 288

I'm Nobody! Who are you?
Are you—Nobody—Too?
Then there's a pair of us!
Don't tell! they'd advertise—you know!

How dreary—to be—Somebody!
How public—like a Frog—
To tell one's name—the livelong June—
To an admiring Bog!

1861

## Questions for **288**

1. According to the **speaker** of the poem, what is the difference between a "Nobody" (line 1) and a "Somebody" (line 5)? Quote the poem's words and **images** to support your answer. What is the effect of the dash followed by the words "you know" (line 4) on your understanding of the relationship between the speaker and the person she is addressing?

2. Why do you think the **speaker** compares a "Somebody" (line 5) with a "Frog" (line 6) and the "public" (line 6) with "an admiring Bog" (line 8)? How does that comparison help determine whether you'd rather be a "Nobody" (line 1) or a "Somebody" (line 5)? What is **ironic** about Dickinson's use of these two words?

**SEE ACTIVITIES, PAGE 108.**

## 341

After great pain, a formal feeling comes—
The Nerves sit ceremonious, like Tombs—
The stiff Heart questions was it He, that bore,
And Yesterday, or Centuries before?

The Feet, mechanical go round—
Of Ground, or Air, or Ought—
A Wooden way
Regardless grown,
A Quartz contentment, like a stone—

This is the Hour of Lead—[1]
Remembered, if outlived,
As Freezing persons, recollect the Snow—
First—Chill—then Stupor—then the letting go—

1862

---

1 lead—a dark, heavy metal that can be used to line coffins.

## Questions for 341

1. Underline the **images** that identify the kinds of "formal feeling" (line 1) the **speaker** of the poem experiences. How do these images and the order in which they appear relate to the images in the poem's last line: "Chill . . . Stupor . . . letting go" (line 13)?

2. What kinds of "great pain" (line 1) do you think the **speaker** might have in mind? Try to recall an experience of your own in which you have felt great pain (for example, the loss of a friendship). Comment on how your experience might help explain the "formal feeling" described in line 1.

## Boat People[1]

After midnight they load up.
A hundred shadows move about blindly.
Something close to sleep
hides low voices drifting
toward a red horizon. Tonight's
a black string, the moon's pull—
this boat's headed somewhere.
Lucky to have gotten past
searchlights low-crawling the sea,
like a woman shaking water
from her long dark hair.

Twelve times in three days
they've been lucky,
clinging to each other in gray mist.
Now Thai[2] fishermen gaze out across
the sea as it changes color,
hands shading their eyes
the way sailors do,
minds on robbery & rape.
Sunlight burns blood-orange.

Storm warnings crackle on a radio.
The Thai fishermen turn away.
Not enough water for the trip.
The boat people cling to each other,
their faces like yellow sea grapes,
wounded by doubt & salt.
Dusk hangs over the water.
Seasick, they daydream Jade Mountain[3]
a whole world away, half-drunk
on what they hunger to become.

1992

1 boat people — people who are so desperate to leave a country in hopes of finding a better life in another land that they pay the owners of small boats, often fishermen, to transport them. The boats tend to be extremely crowded, and the journey risky. After the Vietnam War (1961–1973) many refugees attempted to escape Vietnam for other countries, including the United States.

2 Thai — from Thailand, a country near Vietnam.

3 Jade Mountain — presumably a reference to the eighteenth-century Buddhist Ngoc Son Temple on an island in Haa Kiem Lake in Vietnam. The temple is known for its beauty and peaceful atmosphere.

## Questions for **Boat People**

1. Explain the relationship between the boat people and the Thai fishermen. How does the boat people's luck change in the second stanza?

2. Why are the boat people's "faces like yellow sea grapes, / wounded by doubt & salt" (lines 25–26)? What do they hope for in the future?

## Little Man around the House

Mama Elsie's ninety now.
She calls you whippersnapper.[1]
When you two laugh, her rheumatism[2]
Slips out the window like the burglar
She hears nightly. Three husbands
& an only son dead, she says
*I'll always be a Daddy's girl.*
*Sometimes I can't get Papa's face*
*Outta my head. But this boy, my great-*
*Great-grandson, he's sugar in my coffee.*

You look up from your toy
Telescope, with Satchmo's[3] eyes,
As if I'd put a horn to your lips.
You love maps of buried treasure,
Praying Mantis,[4] & Public Enemy . . .[5]
Blessed. For a moment, I'm jealous.
You sit like the king of the trumpet
Between my grandmama & wife,
Youngblood,[6] a Cheshire cat[7]
Hoodooing[8] two birds at once.

for Ladarius

1993

---

1 whippersnapper — a person, often a young person, who behaves in a fresh, "smart alecky" manner.

2 rheumatism — a disease marked by pain and stiffness in the joints and back.

3 Satchmo — the nickname of Louis Armstrong (1900–1977), a famous New Orleans jazz musician who played the trumpet.

4 Praying Mantis — a "new-wave" British "heavy-metal" band.

5 Public Enemy — a rap band.

6 Youngblood — youth or the practices and ideas of youth.

7 Cheshire cat — the cat in British author Lewis Carroll's children's story, *Alice's Adventures in Wonderland* (1865). The Cheshire cat has a mysterious grin.

8 hoodooing — causing bad luck.

## Questions for **Little Man Around the House**

1. Underline phrases in the first stanza that describe how Mama Elsie feels about her "great- / Great-grandson" (lines 9–10). Circle the poem's **similes** and **metaphors**. How do you think the experiences Mama Elsie describes in lines 5–9 contribute to her feelings toward him?

2. What observations does the **speaker** make about his son (Mama Elsie's "great- /Great-grandson")? What do you think he means when he says, "For a moment, I'm jealous" (line 16)?

**SEE ACTIVITIES, PAGE 108.**

# Slam, Dunk, & Hook[1]

Fast breaks.[2] Layups.[3] With Mercury's[4]
Insignia on our sneakers,
We outmaneuvered the footwork[5]
Of bad angels. Nothing but a hot
Swish of strings like silk
Ten feet out. In the roundhouse[6]
Labyrinth our bodies
Created, we could almost
Last forever, poised in midair
Like storybook sea monsters.
A high note hung there
A long second. Off
The rim. We'd corkscrew
Up & dunk[7] balls that exploded
The skullcap[8] of hope & good
Intention. Bug-eyed, lanky,
All hands & feet . . . sprung rhythm.[9]
We were metaphysical when girls
Cheered on the sidelines.
Tangled up in a falling,
Muscles were a bright motor
Double-flashing to the metal hoop
Nailed to our oak.[10]
When Sonny Boy's mama died
He played nonstop all day, so hard
Our backboard splintered.
Glistening with sweat, we jibed[11]
& rolled the ball off our
Fingertips. Trouble
Was there slapping a blackjack[12]
Against an open palm.
Dribble, drive[13] to the inside, feint,[14]
& glide like a sparrowhawk.
Lay ups. Fast breaks.
We had moves we didn't know
We had. Our bodies spun
On swivels of bone & faith,
Through a lyric slipknot[15]
Of joy, & we knew we were
Beautiful & dangerous.

1992

---

1 hook — a basketball shot made by a player who faces away from the basket and hooks his arm to make the shot.

2 fast break — the moment at which one team grabs the ball and takes it to the other end of the court.

3 layup — a shot made from under the net when the ball bounces off the backboard and through the net.

4 Mercury — ancient Roman god who served as the messenger of the gods and was known for his swiftness.

5 footwork — the use of the feet in a skillful manner.

6 roundhouse — a basketball term that refers to the semi-circle outside the foul lines. A player who makes a basket from this area gets an extra point for his or her team.

7 dunk — to slam the basketball from above through the net.

8 skull cap — a small, close-fitting cap without a brim.

9 sprung rhythm — a poetic rhythm characterized by the use of strongly accented syllables along with an unspecified number of unaccented syllables. The accented syllables stand out.

10 oak — wooden support for the backboard.

11 jibed — in sailing, means when the sail is shifted from one side to the other.

12 blackjack — two cards that add up to twenty-one in the card game of poker.

13 drive — to move rapidly toward the basket.

14 double feint — to make a fake move twice to fool the members of the other team.

15 slipknot — a knot that slips easily up and down the cord or line around which it is tied.

## Questions for **Slam, Dunk, & Hook**

1. Underline phrases that describe the motion and skill of the game. Circle examples of **alliteration**. How does the use of alliteration relate to and emphasize the meaning of the lines in which it is used?

2. What is the **speaker** telling us in lines 35–40 about why basketball is so important to these players?

**SEE ACTIVITIES, PAGE 108.**

## Starlight Scope[1] Myopia[2]

Gray-blue shadows lift
shadows onto an oxcart.

Making night work for us,
the starlight scope brings
men into killing range.

The river under Vi Bridge
takes the heart away

like the Water God
riding his dragon.[3]
Smoke-colored

Viet Cong[4]
move under our eyelids,

lords over loneliness
winding like coral vine[5] through
sandalwood[6] & lotus,[7]

inside our lowered heads
years after this scene

ends. The brain closes
down. What looks like
one step into the trees,

they're lifting crates of ammo[8]
& sacks of rice, swaying

under their shared weight.
Caught in the infrared,[9]
what are they saying?

Are they talking about women
or calling the Americans

*beaucoup dien cai dau?*[10]
One of them is laughing.
You want to place a finger

to his lips & say "shhhh."
You try reading ghost talk

on their lips. They say
"up-up we go," lifting as one.
This one, old, bowlegged,

you feel you could reach out
& take him into your arms. You

peer down the sights of your M-16,[11]
seeing the full moon
loaded on an oxcart.

1992

---

1 starlight scope — telescopic lens on a rifle that absorbs starlight to magnify a target. In this poem the speaker conveys the perspective of someone looking through the lens of the starlight scope so that the figures he sees are like those in a silent movie.

2 myopia — nearsightedness.

3 like the Water God/riding his dragon — a possible reference to a story in Vietnamese folklore about a dragon rising from the water. The dragon is a symbol of the Vietnamese nation.

4 Viet Cong — the Vietnamese enemy that American soldiers fought in the Vietnam War. The scene described here is a typical Viet Cong village with men of all ages carrying food and ammunition to help their village survive. The Viet Cong often disguised themselves as village peasants.

5 coralvine — a tropical vine.

6 sandalwood — fragrant wood from certain Asian trees.

7 lotus — a type of plant that, according to Greek legend, causes dreamy contentment and forgetfulness in those who eat it.

8 ammo — slang term for ammunition.

9 infrared — invisible heat rays below the red end of the visible spectrum used to sharpen an image seen through a lens

10 *beaucoup dien cai dau?* — roughly translated from the French and Vietnamese: Very crazy in the head.

11 M-16 — a lightweight, fully automatic rifle that shoots at extremely high velocity; the standard U.S. rifle used in the Vietnam War.

## Questions for **Starlight Scope Myopia**

1. Find phrases that reveal the conflicting emotions the **speaker** has toward the Viet Cong.

2. Underline the **figures of speech** in the first six stanzas of the poem. What effect do they have in conveying emotion and establishing mood?

# CLASSIC MODELS: POEMS AND QUESTIONS

PHOTO BY LINDSAY ZWICKER

## • BALLAD •

The **ballad** is a **narrative poem** that can be traced back to the oral folk tradition in Europe. Folk tradition was the practice of passing on literature from one generation to the next through song and storytelling. During this period between the fifth and eighteenth centuries, simple, often dramatic stories were passed among people who could neither read nor write.

The key element in the ballad is the use of a narrative and an impersonal or objective storyteller or speaker who relates the story to the general public. **Dialogue** and **repetition** (through **rhyme**, **refrain**, or **diction**) are also prominent features.

The anonymous ballad below was a popular poem/song in medieval England.

### Lord Randal

anonymous

1

"O where ha'[1] you been, Lord Randal, my son?
And where ha' you been, my handsome young man?"
"I ha' been at the greenwood;[2] mother, mak[3] my bed soon,
For I'm wearied wi'[4] huntin', and fain[5] wad[6] lie down."

2

"And wha met ye there, Lord Randal, my son?
And wha met you there, my handsome young man?"
"O I met wi' my true-love; mother, mak my bed soon,
For I'm wearied wi' huntin', and fain wad lie down."

3

"And what did she give you, Lord Randal, my son?
And what did she give you, my handsome young man?"
"Eels fried in a pan; mother, make my bed soon,
For I'm wearied wi' huntin', and fain wad lie down."

4

"And wha gat your leavin's,[7] Lord Randal, my son?
And wha gat your leavin's my handsome young man?"
"My hawks and my hounds; mother, mak my bed soon,
For I'm wearied wi' huntin', and fain wad lie down."

5

"And what becam[8] of them, Lord Randal, my son?
And what became of them, my handsome young man?"
"They stretched their legs out and died; mother, mak my bed soon,
For I'm wearied wi' huntin', and fain wad lie down."

6

"O I fear you are poisoned, Lord Randal, my son!
I fear you are poisoned, my handsome young man!"
"O yes, I am poisoned; mother, mak my bed soon,
For I'm sick at the heart, and I fain wad lie down."

7

"What d'ye leave to your mother, Lord Randal, my son?
What d'ye leave to your mother, my handsome young man?"
"Four and twenty milk kye;[9] mother mak my bed soon,
For I'm sick at the heart, and I fain wad lie down."

8

"What d'ye leave to your sister, Lord Randal, my son?
What d'ye leave to your sister, my handsome young man?"
"My gold and my silver; mother, mak my bed soon,
For I'm sick at the heart, and I fain wad lie down."

9

"What d'ye leave to your brother, Lord Randal, my son?
What d'ye leave to your brother, my handsome young man?"
"My houses and my lands; mother, mak my bed soon,
For I'm sick at the heart, and I fain wad lie down."

10

"What d'ye leave to your true-love, Lord Randal, my son?
What d'ye leave to your true-love, my handsome young man?"
"I leave her hell and fire; mother, mak my bed soon,
For I'm sick at the heart, and I fain wad lie down."

---

Most of the following words come from English or Scottish spellings or dialect from the Middle Ages:

1 ha' — contraction for *have*

2 greenwood — a common name for a woods or forest in the spring and summer when the trees are in leaf (that is, green).

3 mak — old spelling for *make*.

4 wi' — contraction for *with*.

5 fain — dialect for *preferably* or *gladly*.

6 wad — old spelling for *would*.

7 "And wha gat your leavin's"— dialect for *and who got your leftovers*.

8 becam — old spelling for *became*.

9 kye — old spelling for the archaic word for cattle, *kine*.

## Questions on **Lord Randal**

1. Notice that Lord Randal's mother is always the **speaker** in the first two lines of each stanza, and Lord Randal replies in the last two lines of each stanza. What does Lord Randal say has happened to him during his time with his "true-love" (line 7) in the "greenwood" (line 3)? Why does he ask his mother to "mak my bed soon" in the third line of each stanza? How does his mother know the cause of his illness? What are Lord Randal's feelings toward his "true-love" (line 7) as revealed in the last two lines of the poem?

2. How does the use of **dialogue, repetition, consonance,** and **alliteration** contribute to the feeling and impact of the story?

   - Poem for Comparison: Dudley Randall, "Ballad of Birmingham"

# · SYLLABIC POETRY ·

## HAIKU, TANKA, AND CINQUAIN

**Haiku** poems are early Japanese poetry that originated with the introduction of writing in Chinese characters, most likely in the fifth century A.D. In the Japanese tradition, the poems were often sung and had a pattern of dance gestures.

Topics common to early haiku poetry include nature, ceremonies, friends and acquaintances, beauty, love, and death. Many of those topics are still used in the haiku poems that have been written in the twentieth century, including those by American poets.

A haiku poem traditionally consists of 17 syllables or sounds written in three lines with a 5–7–5 pattern. Because the Japanese haiku poems shown here are translated, the number of syllables in English does not follow the traditional syllabic structure.

Variations on the haiku include the **tanka** (thirty-one syllables arranged in a five-line pattern of 5-7-5-7-7). The tanka originated from an early Japanese poetic form called the **choka** and was especially known for its focus on love and nature.

Many modern poets continue to be influenced by the haiku's use of an intensely focused image through which the poem's meaning is implied. Adelaide Crapsey's modern invented form, the **cinquain**, which has five lines with 22 syllables in each line, adapts the short lines and compressed imagery of the haiku and tanka forms.

## HAIKU POEMS FROM THE JAPANESE TRADITION

### untitled haiku

Matsuo Bashō (1644-1694)

Translated by R. H. Blyth

| | |
|---|---|
| The autumn tempest | Inoshishi mo |
| Blows along also | tomo ni fukaruru |
| Even wild boars. | Nawaki kana |

### untitled haiku

Masaoka Shiki (1762–1826)

Translated by R. H. Blyth

| | |
|---|---|
| In a corner of the old wall, | Furukabe no |
| Motionless, | sumi ni ugokazu |
| The pregnant spider. | harami-gumo |

### untitled tanka

Lady Murasaki Shikibu (974–1031)

translated by Kenneth Rexroth

| | |
|---|---|
| Someone passes, | Meguri aite |
| And, while I wonder | Mishi ya sore to mo |
| If it is he, | Wakanu mani |
| The midnight moon | Kumo kakurenishi |
| Is covered with clouds. | Yoha no tsuki kage |

## MODERN VARIATION ON THE JAPANESE HAIKU: THE CINQUAIN

### Triad

Adelaide Crapsey (1878–1914)

These be
Three silent things:
The falling snow . . . the hour
Before the dawn . . . the mouth of one
Just dead.

1934

## Questions on **SYLLABIC POETRY**

1. Circle the dominant **images** in each of the **haiku** and **tanka** poems and in the **cinquain**, the modern variation on haiku. How do the images in each poem relate to each other to create a complete picture? How do these poets use short lines and sharp images to create meaning?

2. Reread Chana Bloch's "Deer in the Bush," A. R. Ammons's "Glass Specialty," and Emily Dickinson's poem 288. Give an example from each poem of **imagery** that is similar to that of the **haiku** or **tanka** form.

## · PANTOUM ·

A **pantoum** is composed of **quatrains** in which the second and fourth lines of each stanza repeat as the first and third lines of the next. This process continues through the last stanza of the poem. The number of stanzas may vary. The pantoum originates from Malayan verse (from Malay in Southeast Asia) and was first brought to the Western world by the French poet Victor Hugo in the nineteenth century. It continues to be a popular form among modern poets, who may vary the words slightly in the repeated lines.

### High School Graduation Pantoum

Joan Logghe (1947– )

The dark boy leans against his pickup truck.
His heart widened into Romeo[1] since he met my daughter.
I say to myself, "It's not worth creating a tragedy."
With the Blood Mountains[2] behind them for Verona.[3]

His heart widened into Romeo since he met my daughter,
a girl pulling him by the arms down the driveway
with the Blood Mountains behind them for Verona,
the wild plum blooming, they will make sour fruit.

A girl pulling him by the arms down the driveway,
not long ago, her arms reached, her face ached red for me.
The wild plum blooming, it will make sour fruit,
Passions so sweet, grape couldn't turn wine without it.

Not long ago her arms reached, her face ached red for me,
crying through play-pen bars as I gardened,
passion so sweet, grape couldn't turn wine without it.
I thinned lettuce, her stomach full of milk and need.

Crying through play-pen bars as I garden.
Time is a rascal magpie pecking at the corn.
I thinned lettuce, her stomach full of absence.
I sat next to her driving, yelling, "Brakes!"

Time is a rascal magpie, exotic in the corn.
A yogi[4] asked, "What if this baby should die?"
I sat next to her driving, yelling, "Brakes!"
My heart beats audibly past midnight curfew.

A yogi asked, "What if this baby should die?
Her tongue is long." He wrote on his slate at Lama Mountain.[5]
My heart beats audibly past midnight curfew.
At Christ in the Desert I cried in the chapel for loss.

Her tongue is long, he wrote on his slate in silence.
She's kissed a boy she loved and some she didn't.
At Christ in the Desert I cried in the chapel for loss.
I sat with older mothers who had moved on.

She's kissed a boy she loved and some she didn't.
The dark boy leans against his pickup truck.
I sat with older mothers who had moved on.
I say to myself, "Let's go. It's not worth creating a tragedy."

1993

---

1 Romeo — a reference to one of the young lovers in William Shakespeare's play *Romeo and Juliet*. In the play, the Montague and Capulet families, who have been enemies for many years, try to stop the romance between their respective children. Their effort ends in tragedy.

2 Blood Mountains — Sangre de Cristo mountain range in southern Colorado and northern New Mexico.

3 Verona — a city in northern Italy that is the setting for Shakespeare's *Romeo and Juliet*.

4 yogi — one who practices yoga, an Indian philosophy that practices strict spiritual discipline to gain control over the forces of one's own being and to attain union with the Universal Spirit.

5 Lama Mountain — presumably a reference to a meditation center in northern New Mexico.

## Questions on **High School Graduation Pantoum**

1. Referring to specific words and phrases, describe the relationship between the mother **(speaker)** and her daughter. What are the mother's fears? Why does she say, "It's not worth creating a tragedy" (lines 3 and 36)?

2. Look carefully at the structure of Logghe's poem. Consulting the information on **pantoum** structure, explain how the slight changes in the repeated lines further the progress of the poem. How do the second and fourth lines in the last stanza help the poem's ideas to come full circle?

As early as the Elizabethan era (the second part of the sixteenth century), English poets used a poem's shape on the page to recreate the topic or idea of a poem. Throughout the history of poetry, poets have used **sound devices** for a similar purpose. The following modern poems use shape or sound or both to illustrate or echo the subject matter of the poem.

## We Real Cool

Gwendolyn Brooks (1917–2000)

*The Pool Players.*
*Seven at the Golden Shovel.*

We real cool. We
Left school. We

Lurk late. We
Strike straight. We

Sing sin. We
Thin gin. We

Jazz June. We
Die soon.

1960

## To a Chameleon

Marianne Moore (1887–1972)

Hid by the august foliage and fruit
  of the grape-vine
  twine
    your anatomy
      round the pruned and polished stem,
        Chameleon.
         Fire laid upon
      an emerald as long as
     the Dark King's massy
   one,
could not snap the spectrum up for food
  as you have done.

1959

### Questions on **SHAPE AND SOUND POEMS**

1. Circle examples of **alliteration, assonance,** and **internal rhyme** in "We Real Cool." How do these sound devices help clarify the meaning of the poem's title?

2. How does the **shape** of "To a Chameleon" reinforce the **speaker's** view of the chameleon's distinctive features?

• Poem for comparison: May Swenson, "How Everything Happens"

# • SONNET •

The **sonnet** originated in Italy in the thirteenth century and was made famous by the fourteenth-century poet Petrarch.

It is a fourteen-line poem in **iambic pentameter** with varied **rhyme schemes** that help determine the poem's structure.

The most common sonnets in the English language follow the structure used by Shakespeare: three **quatrains** (a four-line stanza or section) and a **rhyming couplet** (a two-line stanza or section that rhymes). Each of the quatrains develops one aspect of the sonnet's main idea, and the couplet often provides the conclusion.

Many modern poets vary both rhyme scheme and structure when they use the sonnet form.

## Sonnet 73

### William Shakespeare (1564–1616)

That time of year thou mayst in me behold
When yellow leaves, or none, or few, do hang
Upon those boughs which shake against the cold,
Bare ruined choirs[1] where late the sweet birds sang.
In me thou seest the twilight of such day
As after sunset fadeth in the west,
Which by and by[2] black night doth take away,
Death's second self that seals up[3] all in rest.
In me thou seest the glowing of such fire
That[4] on the ashes of his youth doth lie,
As the deathbed whereon it must expire,
Consumed with that which it was nourished by.[5]
This thou perceiv'st, which makes thy love more strong,
To love that well which thou must leave ere long.

---

1 choirs — the part of a church or monastery where services were sung, often decorated with elaborate carvings of wood or stone in the Middle Ages and Renaissance.

2 by and by — shortly.

3 seals up — encloses.

4 That — as.

5 Consumed with that which it was nourished by — consumed by life which also nourished it.

## Questions on **Sonnet 73**

1. Underline the **images** in the poem that give you clues about the **speaker's** age. What feelings do the images convey about the speaker's attitude toward himself, his situation, and the person he is addressing? What do you think the speaker means by "Death's second self" (line 8)?

2. Place brackets around the poem's main divisions, using the **rhyme scheme** and punctuation to help you find them. Label each division according to its main idea and dominant **images**. How do the images in each division reinforce the main idea of the poem?

• Poem for comparison: Robert Hayden, "Frederick Douglass"

## • VILLANELLE •

The **villanelle** is a French verse form that grew out of the Italian folk song tradition. A villanelle is composed of five **tercets** (three-line **stanzas**) and one **quatrain** (a four-line **stanza**).

The first line of the first tercet is repeated as

- the third line of the second tercet
- the third line of the fourth tercet
- the third line of the quatrain

The third line of the first tercet is repeated as

- the third line of the third tercet
- the third line of the fifth tercet
- the fourth line of the quatrain

### Do Not Go Gentle into That Good Night

Dylan Thomas (1914–1953)

Do not go gentle into that good night,
Old age should burn and rave at close of day;
Rage, rage against the dying of the light.

Though wise men at their end know dark is right,
Because their words had forked no lightning they
Do not go gentle into that good night.

Good men, the last wave by, crying how bright
Their frail deeds might have danced in a green bay,
Rage, rage against the dying of the light.

Wild men who caught and sang the sun in flight
And learn, too late, they grieved it on its way,
Do not go gentle into that good night.

Grave men, near death, who see with blinding sight
Blind eyes could blaze like meteors and be gay,
Rage, rage against the dying of the light.

And you, my father, there on the sad height,
Curse, bless, me now with your fierce tears, I pray.
Do not go gentle into that good night.
Rage, rage against the dying of the light.

1934

## Questions on **Do Not Go Gentle into That Good Night**

1. Who are the four kinds of men the **speaker** describes as those who "Do not go gentle into that good night" (line 1)? Write their names in the margins next to the lines that identify them. With what is the night associated and why do these four kinds of men resist it? In the last **stanza (quatrain)** of the poem, why do you think the speaker asks his father to both "curse" and "bless" him (line 17)? What other **paradoxes** can you find in this poem, and why are they important to the poem's meaning?

2. What are the poem's main ideas? How does the musical quality of the **villanelle** contribute to these ideas?

• Poem for comparison: Theodore Roethke, "The Waking"

## THE FIRST DIMENSION: CREATURES

### SET 1. DISCOVERY

- **Julia Alvarez, "Proof"**
  Write a poem about a fantasy you have had about a place you have seen only in pictures or movies.

- **Chana Bloch, "Deer in the Bush"**
  Write a poem or a short prose narrative about an animal you have observed in the wild or a pet at home. Try to express your feelings about the experience of observing another species in its environment, and whether the creature might—or might not—be aware of being observed.

- **Gene Frumkin, "White Panther"**
  Write a poem or prose narrative about a myth, spirit, or creature you believed in when you were younger, such as the tooth fairy, a unicorn, the abominable snowman, or the Easter bunny. Try to convey how you felt when you discovered the myth wasn't true.

- **Naomi Shihab Nye, "Lost"**
  1. Read flyers and advertisements for lost pets posted in your neighborhood, a local veterinarian's office, or a local newspaper. Write a poem that is an advertisement flyer for a lost pet.
  2. Write a poem from a pet's point of view about being lost.

### SET 2. WONDER

- **A. R. Ammons, "Glass Specialty"**
  Research a Greek myth from a book of mythology or think of a familiar myth or fairy tale you have read or studied. Then write a short poem with a contemporary setting that incorporates allusions from that myth or story.

- **Maxine Kumin, "Credo"**
  Write your own "credo" poem by making a list of all the things you believe in. Then try to find concrete **images** or **figures of speech** to convey your beliefs in an imaginative way. You might want to imitate Kumin's **structure** of **run-on lines** or repeated **images** or write your poem simply in the form of a list beginning with "I believe in . . . ."

- **Nancy Willard, "Aquarium"**
  Write a poem about a creature you have observed in a zoo or aquarium.

## SET 1. CHALLENGE

- **Diane Ackerman, "Patrick Ewing Takes a Foul Shot"**
  Write a poem about your favorite sport as if you are a spectator watching a particularly exciting moment in the game. Use **metaphors** and **similes** to describe the actions of the players.

- **Sandra Cisneros, "Little Clown, My Heart"**
  Draw a picture of your own heart as you imagine it **personified**. Using the images in the picture, write a poem in which your personified heart is the **speaker** of the poem.

- **Robert Francis, "The Base-Stealer"**
  Write a poem or prose **narrative** about a moment in your life when you were "poised between going on and back."

- **Joy Kogawa, "Where There's a Wall"**
  Make a list of the real and imaginary walls in your life. What have they prevented you from doing? Write a poem about your experience.

- **Adrien Stoutenberg, "Sky Diver"**
  Write a poem or prose **narrative** about a moment in your life when you realized the importance of gravity.

- **William Carlos Williams, "The Great Figure"**
  Williams's poem inspired painter Charles Demuth to create a painting titled *I Saw the Figure 5 in Gold* in 1928 (Metropolitan Museum of Art, Stiegletz collection) in response to Williams's poem. Find a picture that you like in an art book or on a postcard, and write a poem focusing on one image in the picture. You may want to look at the reproduction of Demuth's painting in the source mentioned in the footnote on the poem.

## SET 2. CHANGE

- **Maxine Kumin, "Life's Work"**
  Write a poem or essay about a challenge you have faced and successfully met.

- **Sharon Olds, "Liddy's Orange"**
  Write a poem in which you use images of a vegetable or fruit as an **extended metaphor** for a change in your life.

- **Theodore Roethke, "The Waking"**
  This poem is in the form of a **villanelle**. Read about the **villanelle** in **Classic Models** and then write your own villanelle.

- **May Swenson, "How Everything Happens"**
  This is a good example of a **shape poem**. Read about shape poems in the Glossary and then write a shape poem in which the lines are arranged in a shape that imitates or suggests the subject matter of the poem.

## SET 1. FAMILY

- **Rita Dove, "Sunday Night at Grandfather's"**
  Think about your family rituals. You might visit a relative on a regular basis, attend a religious service each week, go to a favorite place for lunch or dinner, or have a special holiday tradition. Write a poem about this ritual, using details and images that tell the reader what you like and don't like about it.

- **Carolyn Kizer, "Parents' Pantoum"**
  1. Write a pantoum of your own, using the format described in **Classic Models**. Read Joan Logghe's "High School Graduation Pantoum" and write an essay comparing the way the two poets look at children from the parents' perspective.
  2. Write a poem or essay contrasting the way you see yourself and the way your parents see you. Before writing, make list of the two **points of view**.

- **Suzanne Rancourt, "Whose Mouth Do I Speak With"**
  Write a poem or prose **narrative** in which you focus on a special treat (such as that received by the children in the poem) that you received from a family member.

- **Dudley Randall, "Ballad of Birmingham"**
  1. Choose a newspaper account about a recent event that involves specific individuals. Write a **ballad** about the event, using **dialogue** and **narrative**, and try to imitate the **verse form** used by Randall. Try to imagine the feelings of the individuals and the "story" behind the newspaper story.
  2. Research project: Look up information on the history of the Civil Rights movement and make an oral presentation to your class on the connection between that movement and Randall's poem. Do you think that the ballad form can be a powerful tool for social change?

- **Ruth Whitman, "Listening to Grownups Quarreling,"**
  Write a poem using **similes** and **metaphors** to convey conflicting emotions in a relationship between two people.

- **Al Young, "Son"**
  In a poem or prose piece describe your room from the **point of view** of someone who doesn't like the way you have it arranged.

- **Eric Chock, "The Immigrant"**
  Bring to class a photograph from the newspaper or a magazine such as *National Geographic* of several people working at home or in factories, fields or other places involving manual labor. Then write a poem based on the following steps:

  - Describe what you see in the picture as if you are a journalist reporting only the visual details of the scene. Do not describe the emotional content of the picture, only physical facts. You may choose to concentrate on just one figure in the picture.

  - Exchange pictures and descriptions with a partner. Write three questions you would like to ask your partner about the laborer in your partner's picture. Your partner should do the same for your picture.

  - Write answers to your partner's questions. Draw on your imagination as well as the facts that the picture reveals.

  - From your answers to your partner's questions directed toward a figure in your picture, write a new description of the picture, one that now reveals emotions, attitudes, and ideas as well as physical details.

  - Turn your description into a poem.

- **Lucille Clifton, "jackie robinson"**
  Choose a personal hero or heroine and look up information about him or her (through library or Internet research or conduct an interview). Then write a poem about that person.

- **Robert Hayden, "Frederick Douglass"**
  Look up information about Frederick Douglass in the library or on the Internet. Choose two images in the poem that you can explain as a result of your research. Write a paragraph discussing these two images.

- **Garrett Hongo, "What For"**
  Using Hongo's poem as a model, write your own "What For" poem. Begin by making two lists of images, one associated with your experiences and one associated with the experiences of a parent or another role model.

- **Cathy Song, "Blue Lantern"**
  This poem employs the technique of **synesthesia** by using visual images to suggest sounds. Write a poem using visual images and figures of speech to convey feelings about sounds and the situations associated with them. Try playing classical music or jazz while you write your poem.

- **Mary TallMountain, "Matmiya"**
  Draw a picture of Matmiya.

## SET 1. EMILY DICKINSON

- **585**
  Write a poem that uses an **extended metaphor** to compare a mode of transportation to an animal. Also use at least one of the following sound devices to enhance the comparison: **alliteration, assonance,** or **consonance**.

- **605**
  Write a poem about an insect you like or dislike or fear. Use **metaphors** to convey your observations of the insect's behavior.

- **288**
  Write a poem about the kind of person you wouldn't want to be by using animal **personification** (such as Dickinson's frog) to represent that kind of person. Use humor to *show* rather than *tell* your preferences.

## SET 2. YUSEF KOMUNYAKAA

- **"Little Man around the House"**
  1. Write a poem about a time when you were jealous of someone in your family or someone outside your family to whom you are/were close.
  2. Write a poem about a relationship between members of two different generations. You may write about members of your own family, or you may choose to imagine the relationship between strangers you observe in a restaurant, grocery store, place of worship, and so on.

- **"Slam, Dunk, & Hook"**
  Choose a sport or physical activity you enjoy and write a poem in which the sport becomes an **extended metaphor** for the way you view yourself. Try to use the technical language of that sport.

# CLASSIC MODELS

Experiment with fixed-form poetry by writing a poem on a topic of your choice. Try to imitate the structure of any of the fixed-form poems in this section: **ballad, haiku, tanka, pantoum, shape or sound poems, sonnet,** and **villanelle**.

## GLOSSARY OF POETIC TERMS

**alliteration** The close repetition of initial letters or consonant sounds for special effect.

*Example:* In "The Immigrant" Eric Chock repeats the *w* sound in "waiting for when she can walk" (line 32) to emphasize the immigrant's patience.

**allusion** A reference to a literary or historical person or subject.

*Example:* In Yusef Komunyakaa's "Little Man around the House" the speaker says his son looks up "with Satchmo's eyes" (line 12). Satchmo is the nickname of Louis Armstrong, a famous African American jazz musician.

**assonance** Repeated vowel sounds in a sequence of words or lines for special effect.

*Example:* In Gene Frumkin's "White Panther" the repetition of the *o* sound in "stony cold" (line 10) emphasizes the sensation of cold that the poem conveys.

**ballad** A narrative poem in which an objective or impersonal storyteller or speaker relates a tale to the general public.

*Examples:* Dudley Randall, "Ballad of Birmingham"; and Anonymous, "Lord Randal," in **Classic Models.**

**choice of words** or **diction** The words a poet chooses for a particular effect.

*Example:* In "Aquarium" Nancy Willard chooses "works out" (line 1) and "clean gym" (line 2) to establish immediately the idea of the frog as an athlete in fitness training.

**cinquain** A modern form of syllabic poetry invented by Adelaide Crapsey. The poem has five lines with 22 syllables in a 2-4-6-8-2 pattern.

**consonance** The repetition of consonants for special effect at the beginning, middle, or end of words.

*Example:* In Maxine Kumin's "Credo" the repetition of the soft *ch, sh, c,* and *s* sounds emphasizes a gentle relationship between the speaker and the bear in "I *c*ede him a *s*wale of *ch*oke*ch*erries in Augu*s*t. / I give the *s*ow and her cub as mu*ch* yardage / a*s* they de*s*ire when our paths inter*s*ect / as doe*s* my hor*s*e *sh*ifting under me" (lines 17-20).

**context** The part of a line or lines of poetry in which a word or passage occurs that helps to explain the meaning of the line or lines of poetry. Context can also be the background circumstances or the situation in which an event occurs. These circumstances or this situation can also help explain the meaning of part or all of a poem.

*Example:* Yosef Komunyakaa's "Starlight Scope Myopia" is set in the context of the Vietnam War. This is made clear by the incident and emotions the speaker describes and specific references such as "an oxcart" (line 40), "The river under Vi Bridge" (line 6), and "Viet Cong" (line 11).

**dialogue** Conversation between characters in a narrative poem.

*Example:* The anonymous ballad "Lord Randal" is composed entirely of dialogue between Lord Randal and his mother.

**extended metaphor** A series of comparisons in which each image develops from the previous one.

> *Example:* Sharon Olds's "Liddy's Orange" uses a series of comparisons between an orange and a thirteen-year-old girl named Liddy to convey the different phases of the girl's development.

**extended simile** A series of comparisons using *like* or *as* in which each image develops from the previous one. The result is one extended, unified comparison of two things.

> *Example:* The second stanza of Diane Ackerman's "Patrick Ewing Takes a Foul Shot" compares Ewing's shooting the ball to emerging from the Caribbean Sea.

**figure of speech** A use of language that calls sharp attention to actions or characteristics in a descriptive piece of writing by saying something in a way that is not literal. A figure of speech compares or contrasts, visualizes, or dramatizes relationships between actions or characteristics.

> *Examples:* **metaphor, extended metaphor, personification,** and **simile** are all figures of speech that you will find in many of the poems in this book. See separate entries for definitions and examples of each of these.

**fixed form** A specific poem form that has a set number and/or specific pattern of elements like lines, syllables, meter, rhythm, and or rhymes.

> *Examples:* The **ballad, haiku, tanka, cinquain, pantoum, sonnet,** and **villanelle**. See Classic Models for examples of each type of fixed-form poem.

**foot** The pattern of accented and unaccented syllables found in a line of verse.

> *Example:* one short beat ˘, one long beat ¯ as in line 1 of William Shakespeare's Sonnet 73,
>
> "That tĭme / ŏf yēar / thŏu māyst / ĭn mē / bĕ hōld."

**form** A general term that refers to the physical pattern and shape that a poem makes on a page. If the form resembles or mimics a specific shape, the poem is frequently called a shape poem.

> *Example:* The shape of May Swenson's "How Everything Happens" resembles the action of a wave, with the ascending lines representing a wave "stacking up" and the descending lines the wave "pulling back."

**free verse** Lines having no specific meter; instead, they resemble natural speech rhythms. Most of the poems in this anthology are written in free verse, a form especially common in twentieth-century poetry.

> *Example:* Chana Bloch's "Deer in the Bush" is written in free verse.

**haiku** A form of poetry that originated in Japan. It is written in three lines with a 5-7-5 syllabic pattern.

> *Examples:* See **Syllabic Poetry** in **Classic Models**.

**iambic pentameter** Meter in which a line of poetry has five beats. (*Penta* means "five" in Latin.) Each pair of syllables has the unaccented beat on the first syllable and the accented beat on the second syllable.

*Example:* Line 2 of William Shakespeare's Sonnet 73 is written in iambic pentameter: "When yellow leaves, or none, or few, do hang."

**images** or **imagery** Words that create mental pictures or other sensory detail.

*Example:* In A. R. Ammons's "Glass Specialty" the image of the "fluttering rival in / the garage window: pecking / as at a nectar of hatred," (lines 4–6) creates a picture of a bird reacting to its reflection in a window.

**irony** A contrast between what is expected and what actually happens in a specific situation; a contrast between what someone says and what he actually means.

*Example 1:* In "Son" by Al Young the speaker tells the adult he is addressing to accept his adolescent's messy room. The reader might expect the speaker, like many traditional parents, to support an effort to have the child clean up his room.

*Example 2:* When the son in "Lord Randal" refers to his "true-love" (line 7), he really means the false woman who has betrayed him by poisoning him.

**kinesthetic imagery** Imagery that conveys the feeling of movement.

*Example:* In Sandra Cisneros's "Little Clown, My Heart" the kinesthetic images in "Backflips snapping open like / A carpenter's hinged ruler" (lines 4–5) convey the movement of an acrobat.

**metaphor** A figure of speech that makes a direct comparison between two different things that have something in common. The words *like* or *as* are not used to make the comparison or show the relationship.

*Example:* In Yosef Komunyakaa's "Slam, Dunk, & Hook" there is a metaphoric comparison between the athletes' muscles and a motor: "Muscles were a bright motor / Double-flashing to the metal hoop" (lines 21–22).

**meter** The pattern of accented and unaccented syllables in a line of verse that contributes to the poem's rhythm. Types of meter:

- iambic - one short beat, one long beat — refer
- trochaic - one long beat, one short beat — careless
- anapestic - two short beats, one long beat — contradict
- dactylic - one long beat, two short beats — stinginess
- spondaic - two or more long beats in succession — doghouse

**narrative poem** The telling of a story in verse, with a focus on a single incident or a series of incidents. A ballad is an example of a narrative poem.

*Example:* Anonymous, "Lord Randal." See **Ballad** in **Classic Models**.

**octave** A stanza that is eight lines in length.

*Example:* See **sonnet** in **Classic Models**.

**onomatopoeia** The use of words whose sound or pronunciation implies their meaning.

*Example:* In William Carlos Williams's "The Great Figure," the sounds of the word *clangs* ("gong clangs," line 10) and the word *howls* ("siren howls," line 11) imply their meanings.

**pantoum** A poem composed of quatrains in which the second and fourth lines in the first stanza become the first and third lines in the second stanza, and so on.

*Example:* See **pantoum** in **Classic Models**.

**paradox** A statement or situation in which some elements that might appear to be contradictory are seen as compatible.

*Example:* In Theodore Roethke's "The Waking," "I wake to sleep" (line 1) is a paradox because the contradictory actions of waking and sleeping are shown to be compatible.

**paraphrase** A "translation" of a line or lines of poetry or prose into one's own words. The paraphrasing or translation should follow the original word order and meaning as closely as possible.

*Example:* The first line of Gary Soto's "Black Hair," "I was brilliant with my body" could be paraphrased as "I felt wonderful about myself in a physical way."

**personification** A figure of speech in which ideas, objects, or animals are given human characteristics.

*Example:* Emily Dickinson's "605" personifies the spider by referring to his "Hands" (line 2) and his "dancing" (line 3).

**point of view** The position or perspective from which the speaker in a poem observes or describes a scene, person, creature, or object. It is from this perspective that the speaker tells the story.

*Example:* The point of view in Rita Dove's "Sunday Night at Grandfather's" is that of a woman reflecting on her childhood experiences.

**quatrain** A stanza of four lines.

*Example:* See **sonnet** in **Classic Models.**

**repetition** The use of repeated words, phrases, or sounds to emphasize their importance to the poem's meaning.

*Example:* In Diane Ackerman's "Patrick Ewing Takes a Foul Shot" the repetition of "packing it" (line 4) and other *–ing* verbs emphasizes Ewing's tension as he prepares to make a foul shot.

**rhyme** (also spelled **rime**) Repetition of sound in accented syllables that appear in similar positions within lines of poetry.

Types of rhyme according to position:

*end rhyme:* at the end of a line of verse

*internal rhyme:* within, but not at the end, of a line of verse

*Examples:* Ruth Whitman uses internal rhyme in "Listening To Grownups Quarreling,": "standing in the hall against the / wall with my little brother" (lines 1–2). The words "hall" and "wall" contain the same *ȯl* sound. Theodore Roethke uses end rhyme in "The Waking" in "slow" (end of line 1) and "go" (end of line 3).

**rhyme scheme** The pattern of rhyme that appears in a verse of poetry. Lowercase letters of the alphabet are used to mark the rhyme scheme.

*Example:* The rhyme scheme for the first four lines of Robert Hayden's "Frederick Douglass" is abaa. The words *beautiful* (line 1), *all* (line 2), and *systole* (line 4) rhyme:

| | |
|---|---|
| When it is finally ours, this freedom, this liberty, this beautiful | a |
| and terrible thing, needful to man as air, | b |
| usable as earth; when it belongs at last to all, | a |
| when it is truly instinct, brain matter, diastole, systole, | a |

**rhyming couplet** A two-line stanza with lines of the same length and rhythm.

*Example:* The last two lines (lines 13–14) of Shakespeare's Sonnet 73 are a rhyming couplet:

This thou perceiv'st, which makes thy love more strong,
To love that well which thou must leave ere long.

**rhythm** The musical movement of a poem created either by **meter** or by the planned arrangement of words similar to natural speech.

**run-on line** A line of poetry that does not end with a natural pause and flows easily into the next line, despite a line break.

*Example:* Maxine Kumin's "Credo" has several examples of run-on lines, such as "their nostrils / level with my mouth" (lines 28–29).

**sestet** A stanza composed of six lines.

*Example:* See **Sonnet** in **Classic Models**.

**shape poem** A general term that refers to the physical pattern or shape that a poem makes on a page. Often poets use a poem's shape to recreate the topic or idea of a poem.

*Example:* See **Shape and Sound Poems** in **Classic Models**.

**simile** A figure of speech that makes a comparison between two unlike objects that have something in common. The comparison is made with prepositions or conjunctions such as *like* or *as*.

*Example:* In Julia Alvarez's "Proof" the speaker compares a woman (named Gladys) to a man in the Bible (Thomas) known for his tendency to doubt: "Only Gladys like doubting Thomas / touched the dots wanting proof / the dog wasn't just another / made-in-the-USA gadget" (lines 10–13).

**sonnet** A fourteen-line poem in iambic pentameter with varied rhyme schemes depending on a poem's structure.

*Example:* See **Sonnet** in **Classic Models**.

**speaker** The narrator or point of view through whom the poet is speaking. The speaker of the poem should not be confused with the poet.

*Example:* In Maxine Kumin's "Life's Work" the speaker reminisces about the dreams of her youth and those of her mother. She addresses the poem to her mother in "Mother my good girl" (line 1).

**stanza** A repeated group of lines (two or more) in a poem. Grouping of lines in a stanza may be determined by form (number of lines, line length, meter, etc.) and content.

**structure** The organizational plan of a poem determined by its development of ideas (content). Structure establishes specific divisions within the poem.

*Example:* Robert Hayden uses a colon to separate the first six lines of "Frederick Douglass" from the last eight lines. In the first part of the poem the speaker discusses freedom, and in the second part he focuses on Douglass.

**symbol** An action, object, person, or situation that has meaning in itself but that also represents something else, such as an emotion or idea.

*Example:* In Suzanne Rancourt's "Whose Mouth Do I Speak With" amber is valuable as a fossil of spruce resin and is sometimes made into jewelry. It also represents a valuable gift that the speaker's father gives his children.

**synesthetic imagery** Imagery in which one type of sensory stimulation evokes another.

*Example:* Lines 10-14 of Cathy Song's "Blue Lantern" ("I dreamed the music . . . blue plate").

**tanka** A form of poetry, particularly Japanese poetry, that is composed of thirty-one syllables in a five-line pattern of 5–7–5–7–7.

*Example:* See **Syllabic Poetry** in **Classic Models**.

**technique** The way in which a poet uses language, structure, verse form, and various poetic devices (such as irony, metaphor, and so on) to create a particular effect in a poem.

**tercet** See **Villanelle** in **Classic Models**.

**theme** The main idea or concept around which a poem develops. The theme is most often not directly stated but only suggested or implied.

*Example:* The theme of Cathy Song's "Blue Lantern" is the beauty and inspiration of a grandfather's flute playing that keeps the memory of his dead wife alive.

**verse form** The structure of verses or stanzas in a poem. Structure is determined by the number and length of lines in each stanza and the use of punctuation in each line.

*Example:* See **Pantoum** in **Classic Models**.

**villanelle** A poem originating from the Italian folk song tradition and composed of six stanzas with a set number of lines and rhyme scheme.

*Example:* See **Villanelle** in **Classic Models**.

# ABOUT THE POETS

**Ackerman, Diane** (1948– ) Born in Waukegan, Illinois, Ackerman has a Ph.D. from Cornell University and has taught at Cornell and Columbia University. She has published several volumes of poetry and essays, often with a strong emphasis on the natural world.

**Alvarez, Julia** (1950– ) Born in New York City, Alvarez returned as an infant to the Dominican Republic, where her father, a doctor, was politically active. The family settled permanently in New York in 1960. Alvarez failed English in her American schools, but, ironically, she now writes exclusively in English. Alvarez has published both poetry and novels, and she has taught in numerous high schools and universities.

**Ammons, A. R.** (1926–2001) Born in North Carolina, Ammons has published more than twenty volumes of poetry and won the 1993 National Book Award for his collection *Garbage*. He has taught at Cornell University.

**Bashō, Matsuo** (1644–1694) A Japanese poet, Bashō is generally recognized as the creator and greatest master of the haiku form. It is believed that he was deeply influenced by Zen Buddhism, a religious movement introduced in Japan in the twelfth century.

**Bloch, Chana** (1940– ) Born in the Bronx, New York, Bloch has a Ph.D. from the University of California and has published numerous books. She teaches at Mills College in Oakland, California.

**Brooks, Gwendolyn** (1917–2001) Born in Topeka, Kansas, Brooks attended art school, eventually turning to the writing of poetry. She won a Pulitzer Prize for her book *Anne Allen* and became Poet Laureate of Illinois.

**Chock, Eric** (1950– ) A resident of Hawaii, Chock writes about contemporary Hawaiian culture. He has edited several anthologies of poetry. Chock coordinates and teaches in the Hawaii Poets in the Schools program in Honolulu.

**Cisneros, Sandra** (1954– ) Born in Chicago of a Mexican father and a Mexican American mother, Cisneros lives in Texas. She has worked as a teacher, a poet-in-the-schools, and as a visiting writer at universities. She has received numerous awards for her poetry and fiction.

**Clifton, Lucille** (1936– ) Born in New York state, this self-taught poet began writing when she was very young. She is the only poet to have two books chosen as finalists for the Pulitzer Prize in the same year. She was a chancellor of the Academy of American Poets in 1999 and currently teaches at St. Mary's College in Maryland.

**Crapsey, Adelaide** (1878–1914) Crapsey is best known for her cinquains, a poetic form she invented as a contemporary version of the Japanese haiku. Her only volume of poetry, titled *Verse*, was written in the last year of her life.

**Dickinson, Emily.** See Close-Ups.

**Dove, Rita** (1952– ) Born in Ohio, Dove has been an English professor and is the author of more than eighteen books. She received a Pulitzer Prize in 1987 for the book-length poem, *Thomas and Beulah*, and served as the American Poet Laureate in 1993.

**Francis, Robert** (1901–1987) Born in Upland, Pennsylvania, Francis graduated from Harvard College and taught at summer conferences and workshops. In 1939 he received the Shelley Memorial Award for writing.

**Frumkin, Gene** (1928– ) Frumkin is a professor emeritus of English at the University of New Mexico, where he taught from 1966–1994. In addition to poetry, he has published fiction, reviews, and criticism.

**Hayden, Robert** (1913– ) The son of poor, uneducated parents, Hayden was a dedicated student who valued the inspiration of the older poets of the Harlem Renaissance and his graduate school mentor, W. H. Auden. Winner of the Hopwood Award for poetry and the Grand Prize for poetry at the Dakar (Senegal) World Festival, Hayden also taught at the University of Michigan.

**Hongo, Garrett** (1950– ) Born in Hawaii, Hongo has published two books and teaches at the University of Missouri. He received a National Endowment for the Arts fellowship.

**Kizer, Carolyn** (1925– ) Currently a resident of Sonoma, California, Kizer attended Sarah Lawrence College and was a fellow of the Chinese Government in Comparative Literature at Columbia University. She was the first director of the Literature Program at the National Endowment for the Arts. In 1984 Kizer received the Pulitzer Prize in poetry for her collection *Yin*.

**Kogawa, Joy** (1935– ) Born in Vancouver, British Columbia, Canada, Kogawa has published four books of poetry as well as books of fiction and children's literature.

**Komunyakaa, Yusef** See Close-Ups.

**Kumin, Maxine** (1925– ) Born in Philadelphia, Kumin lives on a farm in New Hampshire. Recipient of the Pulitzer Prize in 1973, she has published several volumes of poetry on a range of subjects that include nature, farming, motherhood, love, and the Jewish female identity.

**Levertov, Denise** (1923–1997) Born in Ilford, Essex (England), Levertov was educated at home in England before moving to the United States. Her poetry was inspired by such diverse topics as Jewish mysticism and political events such as the Vietnam War.

**Logghe, Joan** (1947– ) Active in New Mexico's poetry renaissance for many years, Logghe was poetry editor for *Mothering Magazine* and has published several books of poetry. She has received a poetry grant from the National Endowment for the Arts. Logghe lives in La Puebla, New Mexico, and teaches poetry workshops throughout the state.

**Moore, Marianne** (1887–1972) Born in St. Louis, Missouri, Moore worked as a writer in New York City where she became editor of the prestigious literary journal *The Dial* in 1926.

Well known for her interest in animals and sports, especially baseball, Moore often uses exotic creatures as metaphors in her poems.

**Nye, Naomi Shihab** (1952– ) A resident of San Antonio, Texas, Nye grew up in St. Louis, Missouri; Old Jerusalem; Jordan; and San Antonio. Her collection of poetry, *Hugging the Jukebox*, was selected for the National Poetry Series, and she received the Lavan Award for poetry from the American Academy of Poets. Nye teaches at the University of Texas and is a frequent guest speaker at international poetry workshops and conferences.

**Olds, Sharon** (1942– ) Born in San Francisco, Olds was the recipient of a National Endowment for the Arts grant and a Guggenheim Fellowship. Her second book of poetry, *The Dead and the Living*, received the National Book Critics Circle Award in 1983. Olds has taught at New York University and Columbia University in New York City.

**Oliver, Mary** (1935– ) Oliver has published seven books of poetry and is a recipient of the Pulitzer Prize for Poetry (1984) and the National Book Award (1992). She teaches at Bennington College in Vermont.

**Rancourt, Suzanne** Born and raised in west central Maine, Rancourt is Abenaki, Bear Clan. She served six years in the U. S. Marine Corps and three in the U. S. Army. Rancourt holds an M.F.A. in poetry from Vermont College and an M.S. in educational psychology from SUNY in Albany, New York. Her work has been published internationally. Rancourt's diverse vocations include education consultant, songwriter, fitness trainer, and percussionist.

**Randall, Dudley** (1914–2000) Born in Washington, D.C., Randall worked as a librarian and was poet-in-residence at the University of Detroit where he also taught English. In the 1960s he founded Broadside Press, dedicated to publishing the work of African American writers. "Ballad of Birmingham" is one of the first poems to be published by Broadside Press.

**Roethke, Theodore** (1908–1963) Born in Saginaw, Michigan, Roethke taught at several colleges, including the University of Washington. His interest in nature and especially in his family's association with forestry and horticulture was a source of inspiration for many of his poems.

**Shakespeare, William** (1564–1616) Born in Stratford-upon-Avon, England, Shakespeare is a world-famous poet and playwright. He is the author of 154 poems and numerous plays including *Romeo and Juliet, The Merchant of Venice, Twelfth Night,* and *A Midsummer Night's Dream.*

**Shiki, Masoaka** (1867–1902) Born in Japan, Shiki is considered the last of the great Japanese writers of the old style of haiku poetry and the first writer of modern haiku. He was particularly known for organizing poetry "parties" at which poets would compete with their individual compositions of haiku.

**Shikibu, Lady Murasaki** (974–1031) A Japanese poet and the granddaughter of a poet, Lady Shikibu was a lady-in-waiting to the empress Akiko and is considered one of Japan's most important writers. She is most famous for her novel *The Tale of Genji*.

**Song, Cathy** (1955– ) Born in Hawaii of Korean and Hawaiian heritage, Song lives in Hawaii and has taught creative writing at various American universities. She was the recipient of the Yale Younger Poets award in 1982.

**Soto, Gary** (1952– ) Born in Fresno, California, Soto teaches at the University of California at Berkeley and has published several volumes of poetry. He was influenced by union organizer César Chavez and by Mexican Americans who promoted Chicano protest literature in the United States.

**Stoutenberg, Adrien** (1916–1982) Born in Minnesota, Stoutenberg attended the Minneapolis School of Art and then became a freelance writer. During her career Stoutenberg wrote at least 40 books, mostly for children, and received numerous awards.

**Swenson, May** (1919–1989) Born in Logan, Utah, Swenson taught at several colleges including Bryn Mawr, the University of North Carolina, and the University of California at Riverside. She published poems in numerous journals and magazines and served as chancellor of the American Academy of Poets from 1980–1989.

**TallMountain, Mary** (1918–1994) Born in Alaska of Athabaskan-Russian and Scotch-Irish ancestry, TallMountain eventually settled in San Francisco. Published in numerous journals and anthologies, her work reflects the influence of her Alaskan childhood and the mountainous terrain along the Yukon River in Alaska.

**Thomas, Dylan** (1915–1953) Born in Swansea, Wales, Thomas published his first book of poetry when he was twenty. Besides poems, he wrote short stories, plays, and film scripts. He is especially known for his narrative poem "A Child's Christmas in Wales."

**Whitman, Ruth** (1922–1999) A longtime Radcliffe Seminars instructor and a member of the faculty at the Massachusetts Institute of Technology, Whitman was a friend and mentor to such female poets as Maxine Kumin and Linda Pastan. She published eight books of poetry, the most well-known of which is *Tamsen Donner: A Woman's Journey*. Whitman received a Bunting Fellowship at Radcliffe and was a Fulbright Writer-in-Residence at Hebrew University in Jerusalem.

**Willard, Nancy** (1936– ) Willard grew up in Ann Arbor, Michigan, and has published eight volumes of poetry as well as several books for children. She teaches English at Vassar College.

**Williams, William Carlos** (1883–1963) Born in New Jersey, Williams practiced medicine in addition to writing poetry. He published several collections, including *Paterson* (1946) and *Spring and All* (1923). Williams's poetry is especially known for its use of the natural, spoken language (vernacular).

**Young, Al** (1939– ) Born in Ocean Springs, Mississippi, Young has written numerous books of poetry. He won an American Book Award for *Musical Memoirs*, published in 1984. Young has received many honors and awards including fellowships from the National Endowment for the Arts and the Guggenheim Foundation. He has been a Wallace Stegner Fellow at Stanford University as well as a Fulbright Fellow. Young lectures widely and lives in Palo Alto, California.

# ABOUT THE AUTHORS

## Carol Clark

A native of New Jersey, Carol Clark received a B.A. with Honors in English from Barnard College (1965) and an M.A. in English Literature from California State University at San Francisco (1977). She has taught middle school and high school English in public and private schools in New York and California for twenty-four years and was English Department Chair at Crystal Springs Uplands School from 1989-1998. A consultant for the Bay Area Writing Project at the University of California, Berkeley, Ms. Clark was elected to *Who's Who Among American Teachers* in 1997 and 1999.

## Alison Draper

Born in North Carolina, Alison Draper earned a B.A. with Honors in English (1975) and an M.A. in Education (1976) from Stanford University. She has pursued post-graduate work at the Breadloaf School of English at Middlebury College. For over twenty years Ms. Draper has taught middle and high school students at The National Cathedral School, The Spence School, San Francisco University High School, and Crystal Springs Uplands School. Most recently she coordinated the English classes in Crystal Springs Uplands' Summer Enrichment program, which is designed for middle-school students from both public and private schools.

# ACKNOWLEDGMENTS

**Ackerman, Diane,** "Patrick Ewing Takes a Foul Shot" from *Jaguar of Sweet Laughter: New and Selected Poems* by Diane Ackerman, copyright © 1991 by Diane Ackerman. Used by permission of Random House Inc.

**Alvarez, Julia,** "Discovery" from *The Other Side/El Otro Lado* by Julia Alvarez. Copyright © 1995 by Julia Alvarez. Published by Dutton, a division of Penguin Putnam Inc. Reprinted by permission of Susan Bergholz Literary Services, New York. All rights reserved.

**Ammons, A. R.,** "Glass Specialty" from *The Really Short Poems* of A. R. Ammons by A. R. Ammons. Copyright © 1990 by A. R. Ammons. Used by permission of W. W. Norton & Company, Inc.

**Bashō, Matsuo,** "untitled haiku" from R. H. Blyth, translator, *Haiku* (Vol. III), Tokyo, Japan: Hokuseido Press, copyright © 1957 and 1952. Reprinted by permission of the publisher.

**Bloch, Chana,** "Deer in the Bush" by Chana Bloch originally appeared in *The Secrets of the Tribe* (New York: Sheep Meadow Press, 1981). Reprinted by permission of the author.

**Brooks, Gwendolyn,** "We Real Cool" from *Blacks* reprinted by permission of The Estate of Gwendolyn Brooks.

**Chock, Eric,** "The Immigrant" by Eric Chock from *Last Days Here*, Bamboo Ridge Press, copyright © 1990. Reprinted by permission of the author.

**Cisneros, Sandra,** "Little Clown, My Heart" from *Loose Woman*. Copyright © 1994 by Sandra Cisneros. Published by Vintage Books, a division of Random House, Inc., and originally in hardcover by Alfred A. Knopf, Inc. Reprinted by permission of Susan Bergholz Literary Services, New York. All rights reserved.

**Clifton, Lucille,** "jackie robinson" by Lucille Clifton from *Good Woman: Poems and a Memoir, 1969–1990*. Copyright © 1987 by Lucille Clifton. Reprinted with the permission of BOA Editions, Ltd.

**Crapsey, Adelaide,** "Triad" from *Verse* by Adelaide Crapsey, copyright © 1922 by Algernon S. Crapsey and renewed 1950 by The Adelaide Crapsey Foundation. Used by permission of Alfred A. Knopf, a division of Random House, Inc.

**Dickinson, Emily,** Poems 585, 605, 288, and 341 reprinted by permission of the publishers and the Trustees of Amherst College from *The Poems of Emily Dickinson*, Thomas H. Johnson, ed., Cambridge, Mass.: The Belnap Press of Harvard University Press, copyright © 1951, 1955, 1979 by the President and fellows of Harvard College.

**Dove, Rita,** "Sunday Night at Grandfather's" from *Museum*, Carnegie-Mellon University Press, © 1983 by Rita Dove. Reprinted by permission of the author.

**Francis, Robert,** "The Base Stealer" by Robert Francis from *The Orb Weaver*, copyright 1948 by Wesleyan University Press. Reprinted by permission of Wesleyan University Press.

**Frumkin, Gene,** "White Panther" by Gene Frumkin originally appeared in *Saturn Is Mostly Weather*. Reprinted by permission of Cinco Puntos Press.

**Hayden, Robert,** "Frederick Douglass" by Frederick Glaysher, editor. Copyright © 1966 by Robert Hayden from *Collected Poems of Robert Hayden* by Robert Hayden, edited by Frederick Glaysher. Used by permission of Liveright Publishing Corporation.

**Hongo, Garrett,** "What For" by Garrett Hongo from *Yellow Light*, © 1982. Reprinted by permission of the publisher, Wesleyan University Press.

**Kizer, Carolyn,** "Parents' Pantoum" from *Harping On: Poems 1985-1995*. Copyright © 1995 by Carolyn Kizer. Reprinted with the permission of Copper Canyon Press, P.O. Box 271, Port Townsend, WA 98368-0271, USA.

**Kogawa, Joy,** "Where There's a Wall" by Joy Kogawa, first published in *Woman in the Woods* by Mosaic Press, ©1985. Reprinted with the permission of the author.

**Komunyakaa, Yusef,** "Boat People" and "Starlight Scope Myopia" from *Dien Cai Dau*, copyright © 1992, Wesleyan University Press; "Little Man Around the House" from *Neon Vernacular: New and Selected Poems*, copyright © 1993, Wesleyan University Press; and "Slam, Dunk, & Hook" from *Magic City*, copyright © 1992, Wesleyan University Press, are reprinted by permission of Wesleyan University Press.

**Kumin, Maxine,** "Credo" from *Looking for Luck* by Maxine Kumin. Copyright © 1992 by Maxine Kumin. Used by permission of W. W. Norton & Company, Inc. "Life's Work" Copyright © 1972 by Maxine Kumin from *Selected Poems 1960-1990* by Maxine Kumin. Used by permission of W. W. Norton & Company, Inc.

**Levertov, Denise,** "The Secret" from *Poems 1960-1967*, copyright © 1964 by Denise Levertov. Reprinted by permission of New Directions Publishing Corp. Reprinted by permission of New Directions Publishing Corp.

**Logghe, Joan,** "High School Graduation Pantoum" from *Blessed Resistance*, copyright © 1999, Mariposa Printing and Publishing, Santa Fe, New Mexico. Reprinted by permission of the author.

**Moore, Marianne,** "To a Chameleon," copyright © 1954 by Marianne Moore, from *The Complete Poems of Marianne Moore* by Marianne Moore. Used by permission of Viking Penguin, a division of Penguin Putnam Inc.

**Nye, Naomi Shihab,** "Lost" from *Fuel*. Copyright © 1998 by Naomi Shihab Nye. Reprinted with the permission of BOA Editions, Ltd.

**Olds, Sharon,** "Liddy's Orange" from *The Gold Cell* by Sharon Olds, copyright © 1987 by Sharo Olds. Used by permission of Alfred A. Knopf, a division of Random House, Inc.

**Oliver, Mary,** "Moles" from *American Primitive,* poems by Mary Oliver. Copyright © 1978, 1979 1980, 1981, 1982, 1983 by Mary Oliver; first appeared in *The Ohio Review*. By permission of Little, Brown and Company (Inc.).

**Rancourt, Suzanne,** "Whose Mouth Do I Speak With" from *Callaloo* 17:1 (1994), 130. © Charle H. Rowell. Reprinted by permission of the Johns Hopkins University Press.

**Randall, Dudley,** "Ballad of Birmingham" by Dudley Randall from *Point Counterpoem* by Dudley Randall and Margaret Danner, Broadside Press, © 1969. Reprinted by permission of Broadside Press.

**Roethke, Theodore,** "The Waking," copyright 1953 by Theodore Roethke, from *The Collected Poems of Theodore Roethke* by Theodore Roethke. Used by permission of Doubleday, a division of Random House, Inc.

**Shiki, Masaoka,** "untitled haiku" from R. H. Blyth, translator, *Haiku* (Vol. III), Tokyo, Japan: Hokuseido Press, copyright © 1957 and 1952. Reprinted by permission of the publisher.

**Shikibu, Lady Murasaki,** "untitled tanka" from *One Hundred Poems from the Japanese* by Kennet Rexroth, copyright © All Rights Reserved by New Directions Publishing Corp. Reprinted by permission of New Directions Publishing Corp.

**Song, Cathy,** "Blue Lantern" by Cathy Song from *Picture Bride*, copyright © 1983 Yale Universit Press. Reprinted by permission of the publisher.

**Soto, Gary,** "Black Hair" from *New and Selected Poems* by Gary Soto © 1995. Reprinted by permission of Chronicle Books, San Francisco.

**Stoutenberg, Adrien,** "Sky Diver" by Adrien Stoutenberg. Copyright © by Adrien Stoutenberg. First appeared in *A Short History of the Fur Trade*, published by Houghton Mifflin. Reprinted by permission of Curtis Brown, Ltd.

**Swenson, May,** "How Everything Happens" from *Iconographs* by May Swenson, published by Scribner, copyright © 1970. Reprinted by permission of R. R. Knudson, Swenson literary executo

**TallMountain, Mary,** "Matmiya" by Mary TallMountain from *There Is No Word for Goodbye* is reprinted by permission of M. Catherine Costello, TallMountain Literary Executor.

**Thomas, Dylan,** "Do Not Go Gentle into That Good Night," by Dylan Thomas from *The Poems of Dylan Thomas*, copyright © 1952 by Dylan Thomas. Reprinted by permission of New Directions Publishing Corp.

**Whitman, Ruth,** "Listening to Grownups Quarreling," from *The Marriage Wig and Other Poems*, Orlando, Florida, copyright © 1968 and renewed 1996 by Ruth Whitman, reprinted by permission of Harcourt, Inc.

**Willard, Nancy,** "Aquarium" from *Water Walker* by Nancy Willard, copyright © 1989 by Nancy Willard. Used by permission of Alfred A. Knopf, a division of Random House, Inc.

**Williams, William Carlos,** "The Great Figure" by William Carlos Williams from *Collected Poems: 1909-1939*, Volume I, copyright © 1938 by New Directions Publishing Corp. Reprinted by permission of New Directions Publishing Corp.

**Young, Al,** "Son" copyright © 1992 by Al Young; reprinted with permission of the author.

# INDEX OF POETS AND TITLES